MY WAY!

LEADERSHIP STYLES OF HISTORY'S 18 MOST PROMINENT DICTATORS
VOLUME 1

ANURAG SIKDER

Invincible Publishers

First published in India in 2019

ISBN : 978-93-88333-45-0

Invincible Publishers

201A, SAS Tower, Sector 38, Gurgaon-122003

Registered Address: Opposite Kasturba Ashram, Radaur, Haryana–135133

Printed in India by Excel Printers Pvt. Ltd.

This book is dedicated to many people. First, to my family, for their unrequited love and unlimited patience. To my close friends and confidants. May we never stop playing and supporting each other. To my advisors, without whom this book would have been a complete mess. And finally, to that invisible guiding spirit who picks me up every time I fall.

INTRODUCTION

"So do not fear, for I am with you; do not be dismayed, for I am your God. I will strengthen you and help you; I will uphold you with my righteous right hand"

Isaiah, 41:10, Old Testament

Much before the English language came into existence and the Book of Genesis was written, an unnamed Sanskrit scholar had conceived the term "*agrani*", which means the one who guides the actions of others by inspiring them with one's own. In other words, *agrani* is the one who leads by example. It was a testament of the kind of leaders who existed at that time. Since language was not widely understood, it was only result-oriented, popular action that could inspire a loyal band of followers.

With the evolution of language and culture, both in depth and number, different people across the world, belonging to different periods of history, defined leadership as per what they observed in their leaders. Aristocrats defined leadership as a direct result of one's "blue blood" or genes. Monarchists believe that leadership qualities exist in a person because of divine sanction. In other words, a leader is one who is executing the will of God. Confucianism expounds the importance of daily living habits and honed skills in the development of a leader. Leninism details a version that is all about collective leadership.

An analysis of the personal narratives of any leader in history can lead to many interpretations of their choices. When those choices are evaluated in light of the circumstances that prevailed, attempting to fit them into any absolute definition of leadership would be an inaccurate inference. When factors such as political situations, economic conditions, social norms and technological advances are considered along with their individual stories, it paints a wholesome picture of their actual narrative. This wholesome picture details the logic guiding their choices. The nature of their choices as a leader and the results of those choices, when structured and analysed, can be fit into certain modern day definitions of leaders. These definitions are better known as leadership styles.

It is the attempt of this book to exemplify the most popular leadership styles through the detailed narratives of selected leaders who have one thing in common: a penchant for violence and cruel punishment. In other words, they are tyrants whose legend precedes them. Their methods were extreme and the number of people who died as a result of their choices is baffling. In some cases, their kill count cannot be estimated with any kind of certainty. But their rule was not short lived. They remained in power for years (in some cases, for decades).

The reason for their sustained rule is different in each case. King Leopold the 2nd could not be ousted because of his "blue blood". Atilla the Hun could not be challenged by the underprepared because of the reign of terror that would follow. In the case of Ivan the Terrible, it was simply because it was more convenient to let him stay in power than let the treacherous local aristocracy take over. Even though scores of people died as a direct consequence of their choices, the masses followed these leaders into the depths of war and destruction. Their style of leadership was befitting the situation they found themselves in. Their stories are ones of successful implementation because of the favourable alignment of the factors that complimented their style.

In this book, the chosen leaders will be analysed within the tenets of the following widely recognised leadership styles:

1. Autocratic Leadership
2. Charismatic Leadership
3. Situational Leadership
4. Strategic Leadership
5. Transactional Leadership
6. Visionary Leadership

While it may be argued that all the chosen leaders should be categorized under the "Autocratic Leadership" style because of their actions and decisions, it is the attempt of this book to look beyond the popular facts and analyse the chronological decision making of each ruler. Not all these leaders were out rightly autocratic leaders. Some were more participative than their popular image would have one believe. Some believed in the informed opinions of a council more than their own wisdom. A telling characteristic of autocratic leadership is to never let authority be delegated. But in the case of some dictators, that is exactly what they did to ease the burden of decision making on them, while retaining the power to correct, amend or reprimand. The in-depth analysis of the narrative of each leader has led to an inference that every dictator's rule may not necessarily be one of outright autocracy. Even though a dictator maybe the final decision maker, throughout history, there have been numerous examples that they may adopt a style that is different from the stereotypical autocratic style that is associated with such leaders.

The 6 dictators in this volume are those who ruled in different parts of the world, from the 5th Century A.D. till the 20th Century A.D... Nearly all the leaders desired a different state of their empire/country/principality than what prevailed before they came to power. But most of them were unable to effect a sustained change because the toll from their acts of cruelty far outweighed their efforts to create positive change. One common attribute of all the chosen leaders was their decision to accept their world for what it is before establishing enough power and influence to change it to what they wanted it to be.

Note:

Each chapter contains a Strength-Weakness-Opportunity-Threat (SWOT) analysis for the concerned dictator. SWOT analysis is a framework used to evaluate a person's competitive position by identifying his/her strengths, weaknesses, opportunities and threats. Specifically, SWOT analysis is a foundational assessment model that measures what a person can and cannot do, and his/her potential opportunities and threats.

A SWOT analysis determine a person's capability, what he/she needs to do to attain their objectives, and what obstacles he/she must overcome or minimize to achieve the desired results. The components of a SWOT analysis are as follows:

- **Strengths** are those areas where one has an advantage over others, or some unique resources to exploit;
- **Weaknesses** are areas where one may be weaker than others
- **Opporutnities** are situations/events/relationships that one can take advantage of to achieve one's objectives
- **Threats** are what may prevent one from achieving one's objectives

Table of Contents

CHARISMATIC LEADERSHIP

ATTILA THE HUN: THE BARBARIAN TYRANT WHOSE ARMY FOLLOWED HIM TO HELL AND BACK

"There is no real world, just the one you create."

-Jolene Stockman

ATTILA THE HUN

(406 A.D. (estimated) – 453 A.D.)

DIARCHIC LEADER OF THE HUNS AND TRIBES OF CENTRAL ASIA (434 A.D.-445 A.D.)

SOLE LEADER OF THE HUNS AND TRIBES OF CENTRAL OF CENTRAL ASIA (445 A.D.-453 A.D.)

In 450 A.D., Attila the Hun, better known as the "Scourge of God" by the Western and Eastern Roman Empire, was at the peak of his power and influence. He was planning his next major conquest, the biggest he had undertaken so far. He wanted the Western Roman Empire to kneel to him and accept him as their ruler. But he had no way of doing this without starting an all-out war. As he sat in his war chamber with his generals, a Roman messenger was brought to him. He had a message from Honoria, the sister of King Valentinan III, Emperor of the Western Roman Empire. She requested Attila's help in freeing her from her forced marriage with a Roman Senator. Attila believed this could mean many things. Was a western woman asking for his hand in marriage? Was this the ploy of Flavius Aetius, Commander General of the Western Roman Empire and his former acquaintance? Or, was this the perfect excuse for him to lay siege to his most coveted enemy? He desired the counsel of his brother, Bleda.

Since 434 A.D., the Huns had two kings: Attila and his brother Bleda. Like the past brother kings, Octar and Rugila, Attila and Bleda put continental Europe, the Visigoths, the Roman Empires and numerous other smaller kingdoms and empires to the sword. All, in varying capacities, had bent to the will of the "Hunnic Brother Kings". If Attila was the "Scourge of God", then, Bleda would be the "Tactical Brain of God". He negotiated tributes with the provinces they conquered which would make the Empire's economy thrive. Tributes would be paid to the Brother Kings in the form of gold, precious stones, crops, weapons, trade sanctions, tax waivers and many other desirable elements of commerce. With the guile of Attila and the influence of Bleda, they expanded the Hunnic Empire from the Great Hungarian Plain to the Balkan territories, up to the fringes of Byzantium and Sicily in Italy. But with prosperity came animosity and jealousy. During their last years together, they argued a lot. They disagreed with each other's plans. Eventually, during a hunting trip in 445 A.D.,

Bleda died under unclear circumstances. Attila laid his brother to rest with the highest honours.

Bleda was the voice of reason to Attila. Now, he was the sole figurehead. In 447 A.D., after 2 years of trying to appoint a worthy successor, Attila came to the conclusion that he could not trust anyone. He decided to become the sole ruler with his council of generals and kings of his vassal kingdoms. He knew Bleda would have asked to be patient. Bleda would have told him to find out why she chose the empire's most capable enemy as her saviour without accounting for the war it would bring? Bleda would have construed this as an act to weaken their presence within their own kingdom, leaving it open to attack from the numerous other enemies of the Hunnic Empire. But he wasn't there to guide Attila or negotiate with Flavius Aetius or King Valentinian III. As the message from Honoria began to frustrate Attila, he took the course of action that he was most familiar with. He ordered the messenger be tortured to find out the true intention behind this message. While history is unclear about what the messenger had told him, Attila sent word to the King that he is coming to Honoria's aid and upon his betrothal to his sister, he would take half of the Western Roman Empire as dowry for the marriage.

After 2 years of continuous marching, numerous battles, destruction of numerous provinces, in 452 A.D., Attila and the Huns were standing at the door of the Western Roman Empire. With an army of soldiers and archers larger than any other army known to man, Attila had come to claim what he believed to be rightfully his. His army had inbred hatred for the Romans. The messenger from King Valentinian III came to Attila and his horse-mounted entourage. Attila ordered the messenger be decapitated and sent back to the King. Many considered this to be a questionable act and the messenger should have been spared. But Attila was incensed with power and rage by this point. All he saw was the conquest of Rome with the heads of Aetius and Valentinian on a pike, at the gates of Rome. Soon, it would become clear whether Attila, the greatest commander of the Hunnic Horde, was truly the Scourge of God, as he had been so fearfully named.

THE HUNNIC EMPIRE BEFORE ATTILA BECAME KING

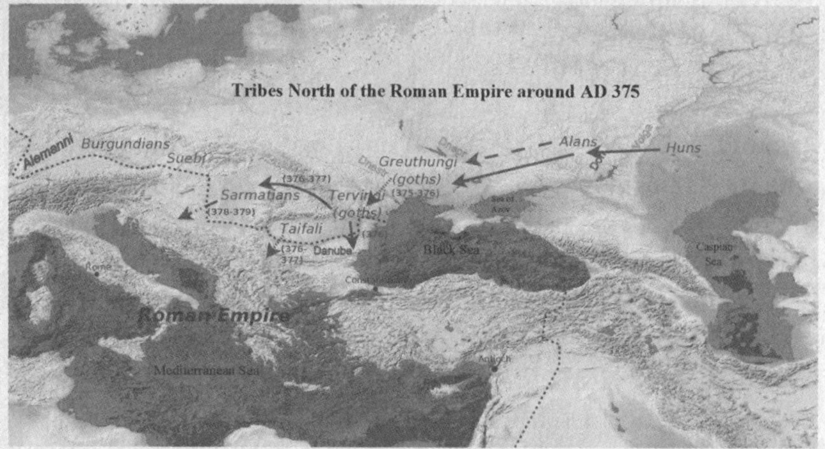

The first time the presence of the Huns had been noted was by geographer Ptolemy during the 2nd century A.D., when he was noting the people of the Eurasia steppe. In his notes, the Huns were only mentioned fleetingly as a simple agrarian race, raising simple crops and leading a simple life. But as time went on, the Huns became more than farmers. By the 350 A.D., they were a collective of pastoral warriors, i.e. their primary form of nourishment was meat and milk from the animals they raised. They wielded javelins and had the first known horse-mounted archers of the human race. The Hunnic people, although firmly camped on the beaches and pastures around the Caspian Sea, were convinced of their abilities to expand their empire.

In the early part of the 5th Century, before Attila, the Hunnic tribe was a relatively small collection of warriors, who had marched out of Central Asia, looking to expand their ranks by harmonizing with other tribes of the surrounding areas. They had chiefly come from North of the Caspian Sea. They had marched to the west, towards Rome and Constantinople. The Hunnic army was sizeable but not large enough to undertake conquests. Under the command of the capable brother Kings, Rugila and Octar, the Huns had waged war primarily against the Ostrogoths (North of the Black Sea) and Alans (Iranian nomads).

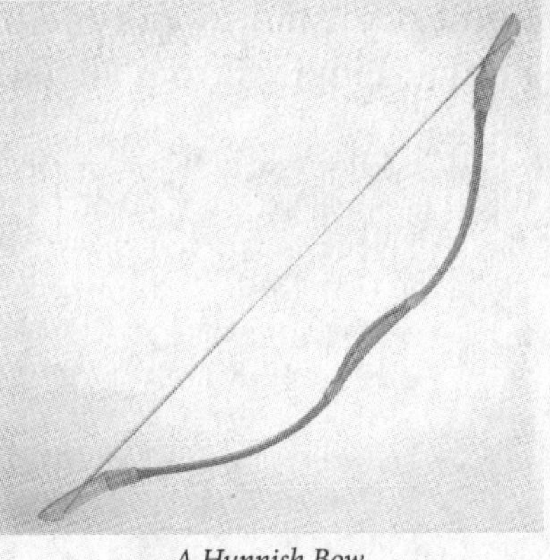

A Hunnish Bow

There had been attempted raids from the neighbouring tribes in the past. Under the diarchy of Rugila and Octar, all of it was put to a firm end. The Huns not only repelled the attack but they were able to secure tributes from the invaders, in exchange for security and peace.

Soon, the instructions to the households of the Huns were no longer just to harvest crops and maintain animal stock. It was also to prepare the young boys at home to wield javelins and basic weapons. Preparations were made to travel east and conquer lands up to the extent of the Danube River. Once there, they destroyed the Gothic Kingdoms and drove the surviving Goths to the fringes of the river. The Goths were forced to cross over into the European lands ruled by the Romans. Rugila was the ruler of the Eastern Hunnic Empire and Octar ruled the Western Empire. Once militaristic supremacy had been established, arrangements were made for the rest of the Hunnic populace to occupy the conquered lands and provinces. It was during this time the practice of taking prisoners of war had begun. A prime example was that of Flavius Aetius, a Roman General, who had been kept captive for many years. Whether it was decision made by Rugila or Octar is not clear. But they learnt much about

Rome, Constantinople and the might of Eastern and Western Roman Empires from General Flavius.

General Flavius Aetius

In 410 A.D., the news came that the Visigoths (known mercenaries of the Goth Kingdoms) had laid successful siege to Rome and had proceeded to loot the capital of the Western Roman Empire. Word about this spread quickly and the Huns were buzzing about the chance to overthrow Rome. But both Kings, after consulting with General Flavius, quelled this excitement by maturely stating their need of the hour was to consolidate power and not waste resources on a hasty and dangerous mission. Soon, General Flavius was allowed to return to Rome by the brother Kings as he promised to speak to the new Emperor of the Western Roman Empire (King Valentinian the 3rd) and make favourable peace terms between the Romans and Huns.

In 430 A.D., Octar stepped away from the position of King, leaving Rugila as the sole leader of the Huns. For the next 5 years, Rugila took two young brothers, Attila and Bleda under his wing. Their exploits were widely spoken about. It was time to prepare for the next generation and Rugila taught them the ways of a Hunnic ruler. These 5 years were a time of relative peace, as an understanding had been made with Rome and Constantinople where 350 pounds of gold had to be given to the Huns every year and they would stop their repeated incursions across the Danube. But in 435 A.D., Rugila tragically passed away and his troops were reeling under a plague that had hit the army.

THE RULE AND LEGACY OF ATTILA THE HUN

MISSION: To unite the tribes of Central Asia and Eastern Europe into a formidable tribal confederation

The Empire of Attila and the Huns

Attila's date of birth is a topic for debate. Some scholars say he was born in the last decade of the 4th century A.D., while others claim he was born in the first decade of the 5th century, specifically 406. If the year is believed to be 406, then he would have taken the throne at the age of 28. As he was raised at a time of rapid change, he learned to adapt quickly to new situations. Along with his brother Bleda, he plotted how to consolidate all the provinces and tribes in the Great Hungarian Plain, Eastern Europe (East of the Danube River) and Central Asia (North and West of the Caspian Sea). With Bleda at his side, he would reign down barbaric terror upon the enemies in the West and North. His brother would negotiate and establish the tributes from the conquered provinces while they quivered under the fear of incurring the wrath of Attila, now better known as the "Scourge of God".

The rule of Attila the Hun is divided into 2 parts. The first part is his diarchy with Bleda. The second part is his sole dictatorship, after Bleda's death.

The First Half

In 434 A.D., King Rugila died after being struck a bolt of lightning.

The Hunnic army was hit by a plague and many soldiers had died while advancing to Constantinople. King Theodosius II, Emperor of the Eastern Roman Empire, saw this as divine intervention to stop the advance of the Hunnic horde. The Huns had not crossed the Danube River and Flavius Aetius had returned from his exile among the Huns after learning much about them and earning their respect. Aetius was reinstated as the leader of the Western Roman Empire's army and he would meet the Huns in the battlefield again, albeit under a new ruler.

POLITICAL CLIMATE OF THE HUNNIC EMPIRE

Political State: Tribal confederation under the undisputed rulers, Attila and Bleda. After Bleda's death, Attila became the sole ruler.

Geographical Division: Polity was divided between north, south, left and right. It is speculated that a big district in the Great Hungarian Plain served as the seat of the Hunnic Empire.

Listed Tribes: The united tribes were the Gepids, Ostrogoths, Rugians, Scirians, Heruls, Thuringians, Alans, Burgundians and many other lesser known tribes.

Leader Status: Attila the Hun was the "ruler of the land" and his instruction was the "law of the land".

Meritocracy was promoted: In the Hunnic society, because there were no aristocrats or monarchs, meritocracy was promoted to recruit the best for all kinds of roles.

When Rugila died, there were cries to appoint Attila and Bleda as the Brother Kings of the Huns. It wasn't just because of lineage though. In past battles, both brothers had shown their skills as commanders and skilled warriors. They had fought side by side in the battles for Greuthungi, Tervingi, against the Sarmatians and the Burgundians. In many quarters of the army, they were regarded as the great rulers who would bring prosperity and sustained glory to the growing Hunnic Empire.

After they took the throne, the first order of business was to expand the army by recruiting the troops from the lands

Solidus Coin

and provinces they had already annexed. They came to favourable terms of understanding with the Ostrogoths and the Alans, who remained loyal to the empire till Attila's death. Numerous other tribes pledged their loyalty to Attila and Bleda, many out of fear of what would follow if they would not bend to their will.

Attila's demand for loyalty was evident right from the start. As the first objective of their rule, they had to strike unprecedented fear in the hearts of both the Eastern and Western Roman Empire. Knowing King Theodosius II to be a leader of weak will, the Brother Kings coerced the King to sign the "Treaty of Margus" (signed in Margus). According to the treaty, the Huns would not destroy Constantinople (capital of the Eastern Roman Empire) in exchange for 700 pounds of gold, opening Roman markets to Hunnic trade, a ransom of 8 gold pieces per Roman soldier and the return of all Hunnic refugees (even defectors and traitors). Within the empire, Attila set an example of all the defectors in his own way through decapitation, skinning bodies and execution by dismemberment. His followers saw this and remembered the punishment for desertion. The tribute from the Eastern Romans would do well to fill their coffers, further strengthening the conquest. Under Attila and Bleda, for the Huns, securing a tribute was just as important a symbol of superiority as territory.

Once the armed forces had been expanded and their loyalty ensured, Attila plotted with Bleda to expand their empire in other parts. The peace with the Romans had to be given a chance to thrive (especially because of the favourable tribute they would receive every year) before a better opportunity presented itself to attack them again. They turned their attention eastward and ravaged the tribes there. Once they had become numerically strong enough, Attila set his sights on the Sassanid Empire, better known as the Neo-Persian Empire. Their influence on south-eastern Europe and Central Asia was strong. The Brother Kings decided to approach them from Armenia as it was located at a strategically advantageous point for them. Attila and Bleda, brimming with confidence marched their troops into Armenia hoping to repeat history (the first ravaging of Armenia had happened under the rule of their uncle, Rugila) and penetrate as far south as possible. But here, they would face one of their worst defeats as commanders of the Hunnic horde.

ECONOMIC PROFILE OF THE HUNNIC EMPIRE

Primary work: Hunting, crop farming and animal herding

Major Trade(s):

a) Raising and selling horses

b) Fur Trading

c) Securing tributes from conquered tribes and Kingdoms

Major Trade Routes: The Black Sea region and the bordering territories of both the Eastern and Western Roman Empires

Alternative Trades:

a) During conquests, looting and pillaging were common

b) Ransoming prisoners of the Roman Empire and selling slaves to the Persian Empire

Trading currency: Solidus (Gold)

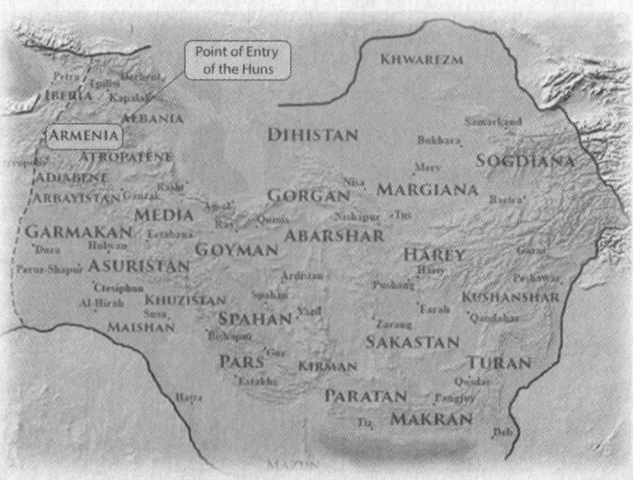

The Sassanid Empire

Emperor Theodosius II

Attila and Bleda had invaded one of the strongest empires in the world. In their youthful hastiness, they had underestimated their enemy and the Huns were swiftly dealt with in Armenia. In less than 6 months, the Brother Kings retreated back to their homeland.

When they returned, they learnt that the Romans had not paid their tribute nor had they returned the traitors. Attila was infuriated further when he learnt that the bishop of the city of Margus had crossed the Danube and robbed the burial treasures from Hunnic graves. In order to re-establish their dominance, the Brother Kings decided to wage war on the Eastern Roman Empire immediately. The Romans were slow to react. The cities of Margus, Singidunum and Viminacium were completely destroyed. Till 443 A.D., the battle between the 2 empires raged because of the Roman's repeated default in paying the tribute. By the autumn of the same year, the cities of Sardica, Philippopolis and Arcadiopolis had been completely sacked. They reached the capital city of Constantinople and defeated the Imperial army on the outskirts of the city. But the city was well defended, so Attila and Bleda moved southward and began razing the cities there. Finally, at Chersonesus, Emperor Theodosius forfeited and accepted defeat.

The tribute: immediate payment of 6000 pounds of gold, annual payment of 2100 pounds of gold, and the immediate return of all Hunnic traitors. This was called the Peace of Anatolius. The Brother Kings marched back home with the greatest plunder ever seen by the Huns. Before this, they were already legends. Now, they had become demigods.

The Second Half

Till 445 A.D., Attila and Bleda had been undisputed rulers for 2 years. Even though, they had fought smaller battles across the fringes of the empire, their might had not been tested, ever since their victory over Theodosius and the Eastern Roman Empire. They both quarrelled about many things, future conquests, each other's halves in the empire, among other petty things. Attila was not the one to back down and neither was Bleda. One evening, they went on a hunt together. The accounts on what happened that day have differed throughout history. Some say, Bleda tried to kill Attila and in retaliation, Attila plunged his sword deep into Bleda's chest. Others say, Attila challenged Bleda to a duel and after a gruelling battle, Attila's sword pierced Bleda's heart. Knowing their respect for one another, Attila and Bleda would have appreciated a good battle if it was one. Regardless of which story is true, Attila came out victorious and from then on, became the sole ruler of the Hunnic Empire.

Attila ensured Bleda was buried with full honours and according to the traditional practices for a fallen leader. This was followed by a feast in the name of Bleda which was attended by many of the Hunnic Empire. The night was filled with merriment and debauchery as was the custom of the Huns. Stories were told of Bleda's cunning ability. Promises and pledges were made to Attila's continued legacy as the greatest king of the Hunnic horde. News of Bleda's death spread throughout Europe and China with many hoping that this would weaken Attila as he would now be without his trusted negotiator and counsellor.

THE HUNNIC EMPIRE'S SOCIAL NORMS

Living Status: Nomadic race

Major religion(s): Tengrism, which included Animism, Shamanism and Monotheism

Language: A mix between Turkish and Mongolian

Common Practices: Artificial cranial formation to "beautify the human head"

Marital System: Acceptance of multiple spouses for men and women

Education: Children were raised and educated by the community, not individually.

According to the Roman historian Priscius, the night Bleda was buried and the feast was conducted, Attila had a dream that an old man had come to him and given the Sword of Mars, the weapon of the Roman God of war. The next

A Hunnic horse mounted archer

morning, when Attila woke from his slumber, a shepherd came to the mighty king and told him how a calf had cut its leg on a blade. Upon searching for the blade in his farm, he had found a sword. When he presented the sword, Attila considered this the fulfilment of a divine prophesy. He had been chosen to wield the sword and he believed that his reign has now been blessed by the Roman Gods as well. Word of this quickly spread through the army and the empire. It was commonplace to believe that they were now being led by the hand of God. Attila was no longer a demigod. According to the Huns, he was the reincarnation of all the Gods they prayed to.

In 447, Attila turned the attention of his Huns back towards the Eastern Roman Empire. Their invasion, led by Attila, of the Balkans and Thrace was a bloody massacre. In Thrace, approximately 70 cities had been destroyed. The Eastern Roman Empire was already beset by internal problems, such as famine and plague, as well as riots. A series of earthquakes in Constantinople that had broken the walled fortification of the city. A last-minute rebuilding of its walls saved Constantinople. Victory over a Roman army left the Huns virtually unchallenged in Eastern Roman lands and they raided as far south as Thermopylae. Only disease forced them to retreat,

THE HUNNIC EMPIRE'S TECHNOLOGICAL ADVANCES

Materials: Mainly timber and basic metal

Main weapons: Swords, Mailles, Langseax, "Hunnish Bow" and Lances

Communication: No long range communication mechanisms

Stock Storage: No food storage mechanisms

Portrait of a typical South Asian tribesman

and the war came to an end in 449 A.D. with an agreement in which the Romans agreed to continue paying Attila an annual tribute of 2100 pounds of gold without any scope for default. This was called the Second Peace of Anatolius. If these terms were broken, Attila swore to return without the intention of negotiation.

By now, Attila had realized that war was not the solution to his problematic relations with the Eastern Romans. He dispatched an embassy to Constantinople, led by the Hunnic commander Edeco. While in Constantinople, the Romans plotted to assassinate Attila and wanted Edeco to play the role of facilitator. In return, he would be bathed in gold and estate. Edeco agreed, but upon returning to Attila's camp (with the Roman ambassadors) he told his King of the plans of the Romans. In an unprecedented act, Attila chose not to act and let the proceedings go on without any hiccups. When the ambassadors had reached Constantinople and sent their emissary with Edeco's bribe, the Roman official arrested and put in chains. Instead of executing the messenger and sending his remains back to the Romans, the bribe gold was sent back with a message for Theodosius "to be careful whom he tries to betray". The Emperor, from then on, paid their tribute on time and did not attack the Huns again. The barbarian King had proven his mettle as a gritty negotiator. The assumption he would weaken because of Bleda's passing had been proven a misconception.

Attila's words were the law of the land. He was the undisputed authority in Eastern Europe, stretching from the Great Hungarian Plain till China. His legend was well travelled and no one wanted to cross paths with Attila or any of his Huns. In the years after Bleda's death, he had remembered the lessons of his brother. He was a charismatic leader, cunning negotiator as well as a brutal executioner. As per the situation, Attila would mould himself into the required character mould. But when the chance to rule the largest empire in the world presents itself, few would be able to resist the temptation to rely on their most basic instincts, especially during one of history's most savage and unpredictable periods.

By 450 A.D., Attila and General Flavius Aetius (commander of the Western Roman Army and Attila's acquaintance), were negotiating the succession of a new Frankish ruler. Attila supported the elder son of the reigning king, while Aetius supported the younger son. While they took a decision on the matter, the Franks were at civil war. Because of the increasing disagreement, respected friends were turning into enemies. Each had their own Kingdom's best interests at heart. Attila was growing increasingly frustrated with the Roman General and his Kingdom's arrogance towards the Huns. The tensions between them were rising. He wanted to depose General Flavius and begin marching to Rome. By conquering Rome, Attila would be the rightful ruler of the largest Kingdom ever known. It would also be the longest campaign he had ever undertaken. For Attila, from the time of his uncles Octar and Rugila, Rome was the final frontier for the Hunnic people. When he told his generals of his plan to invade Rome, they immediately began preparations. For them, they believed in Attila and his unfailing ability as a great ruler.

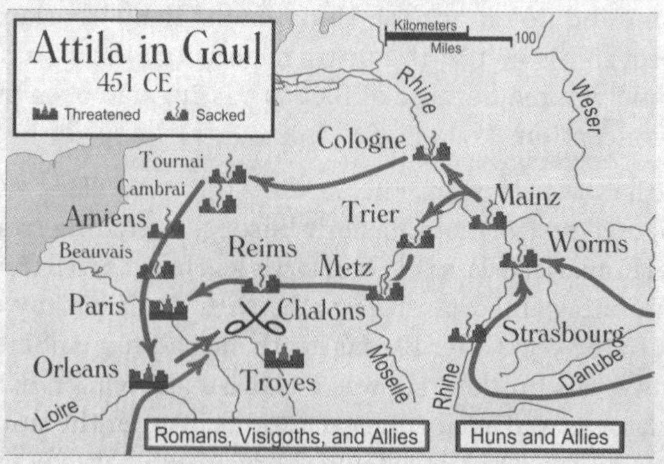

Attila's advance to Rome, through Gaul

While civil war raged in the Frankish Kingdom, Attila assembled his troops to begin a slow yet steady incursion. Starting with Gaul, he slowly advanced towards Rome. He gathered the troops of his vassals- Gepids, Ostrogoths, Rugians, Scirians, Heruls, Thuringians, Alans, Burgundians, among others–and began his march west. In 451 A.D., he set out for Gaul and arrived in Belgica with an army of half a million strong. Attila's army smashed through Germany, causing widespread panic and destruction. In France, he captured Metz, Rheims, Paris, Troyes and finally, Orleans. At Orleans, on the horizon, Attila saw the face of his old friend and new foe, General Flavius Aetius. He, along the Visigothic King Theodoric awaited him, to quell the Hunnic advance. Attila promptly commanded his troops to fall back to the Catalaunian plains, where the legendary "Battle of Catalaunian Plains" was fought.

Attila's battle line contained his own Hunnic warriors in the center, with Ostrogoths and Germans at the flanks. On the other side of the field was Flavius Aetius's army, with his Romans at his left flank and Theodoric's Visigoths on the right. The battle raged initially but came to a stalemate and by night both sides withdrew to their camps. The decisive event actually happened the next day when the Visigoths discovered that their king had, had been killed. Infuriated, they surrounded Attila's camp. However, General Flavius Aetius realized it was unwise to destroy the Huns. In doing so, it would mean the rise of other barbarians. Namely the Visigoths, whom he'd always despised. The Huns were his old allies. He talked the Visigoths out of attacking, and allowed Attila to freely retreat. From the Roman General's point of view, the best outcome had occurred: King Theodoric died, Attila was in retreat, and the Romans had the benefit of appearing victorious.

The Huns at the Battle of the Catalunian Plains by Alphonse de Neuvile

With the Eastern Romans, under their new Emperor Marcian, causing annoyance for the Huns on the Danube River and having ceased paying their tribute to Attila, Attila and the Huns should have retreated to strengthen their hold on his long standing enemy. Instead, the defeat the Battle of the Catalaunian Plains was damaging to Attila's reputation and his larger-than-life ego. The "Scourge of God" now had only one mission: conquer Rome.

Later in the same year (450 A.D.), Honoria, the sister of Valentinian III, Emperor of the Western Roman Empire, had sent a cryptic message to Attila. She requested his help in freeing her from her forced marriage with a Roman Senator. Seeing this as the perfect excuse to march to Rome, Attila assembled his remaining troops and marched again. This time across the Alps. Under the garb of still fighting for the honour of his future wife, Honoria, Attila caught the Romans completely off guard when he appeared suddenly in Northern Italy. Attila stormed the walls of Aquileia, Vicetia, Verona, Brixia, Bergomum, and Milan, massacring the population and destroying the cities completely. His next target was the city of Ravena, where Emperor Valentinian III lived. Attila sent word to the King that he is coming to Honoria's aid and upon his betrothal to his sister, he would take half of the Western Roman Empire as dowry for the marriage. As news of this advance reached the ears of the King, he broke into a panic.

Honoria, sister of King Valentinian III

Promptly, Emperor Valentinian III fled for Rome from Ravena. Even though the Huns were met with stiff resistance, they maintained their charge on Rome. Emperor Valentinian III, his mother and members of his clergy spent most of their time in Rome praying. The Pope, Pope Leo I, insisted that Attila will be punished for his atrocities against the empire and God. It would be divine justice for Attila and his army.

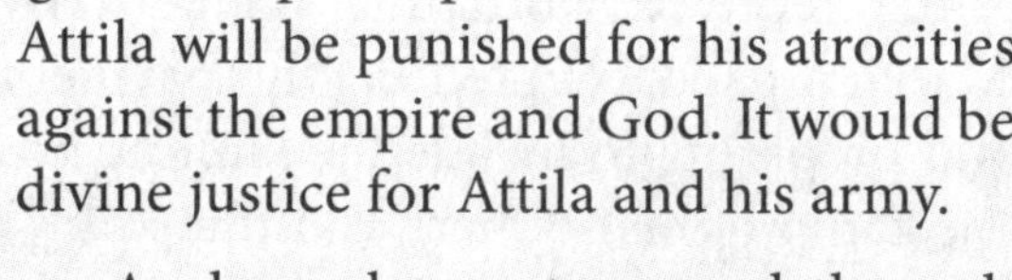

Emperor Valentinian III

A plague began to spread through the Hunnic army. This was not by divine intervention, as the church and the Pope proclaimed. In 451 A.D., Italy had suffered a devastating famine whose effects were being felt in the following year as well. In 452 A.D., the produce had improved, but Attila's brazen "scorched earth" policy had effectively destroyed any increments in production. He soon ran out of nourishment for his troops and they had to survive on whatever they found. The Hunnic army was also feeling the effects of the 2-year long continuous march. Attila was advised to stop and treat the diseased. But believing the momentum was in their favour, he kept his charge going.

Roman General Flavius Aetius too had lost many men in the Battle of the Catalaunian Plains (the understanding with the Visigoths had also fallen through) and was unable to stop the Hunnic advance. He told Emperor Valentinian III that he must negotiate with Attila and put an end to this devastating war. But the King feared the savage King more than he feared death. He would not face him. The King pleaded to the Pope to negotiate with Attila on his behalf and save the Empire. After much resistance, the Pope acceded. Accompanied by the senate's best negotiators, they planned to meet with Attila and come to an agreement. But the meeting never happened.

During the last days of the march to Rome, the Hunnic army was rotting because of plague and famine. Honoria, who had been sent into exile by her brother (who initially planned to execute her for her betrayal), had renounced her allegiance to Attila. Before his meeting the Pope and his counsellors, Attila received word that the Eastern European Emperor Marcian had defaulted on the payment of their tribute and was preparing to invade the Hunnic homeland. He looked at the camp of his soldiers and the paltry conditions they were living in. Food had become scarce and disease was widespread. The troops were growing tired. Attila had a decision to make. In his conference with his generals, he confessed his desire to end the conquest and return home. And so, the Huns turned back and headed towards the Danube River to quell Marcian's invasion. Emperor Valentinian and the Pope considered this divine intervention as a sign, indicating the end of Attila's reign.

STRENGTH-WEAKNESS-OPPORTUNITY-THREAT (SWOT) ANALYSIS OF ATTILA THE HUN

STRENGTHS	WEAKNESSES
1. **"The Scourge of God"**: Building on a reputation of fear and barbarianism, Attila was given the cognomen "The Scourge of God". 2. **Visionary:** Along with Bleda, he wanted to continue the work done by their uncles to unite the nomadic tribes into a tribal confederation. 3. **Adaptable**: As the years of his conquest rolled along, Attila adapted to newer enemies and even took prisoners instead of slaughtering everyone to maintain bilateral relationships with his enemies and other empires. 4. **Authoritarian**: From his ascension to the throne till his death, Attila was always an authoritarian who was feared and respected (not necessarily in equal measure). 5. **Action-oriented**: Attila was always one to let his actions speak louder than his words.	1. **Gluttonous**: Attila was known to indulge in excess and encouraging his war party to do the same. Rape, mass killing and violent sackings were common during his reign 2. **Blind rage**: A key weakness of Attila was his blind rage that led to many rivalries in the future 3. **Non-diplomatic**: Diplomacy was never a part of his agenda. 4. **Non-inclusive leader**: Attila only consulted those he deemed fit to be in his presence. 5. **Greed**: Attila's insatiable greed served his people well, but it also took a great toll on his relationships and his decision making. The most glaring example is the death of his brother, Bleda, with whom he quarrelled frequently before his death about the extent of their power on certain territories.
OPPORTUNITIES	**THREATS**
1. **United Tribal Confederation:** To unite the nomadic tribes of eastern Europe and central Asia, to form the largest known empire in the world at that point in time. 2. **Trade expansion:** Trade expansion across the Western and Eastern Roman Empire by establishing guaranteed tributes from the different lands and provinces captured by the Huns. 3. **Undisputed Kingship:** In a time of fragmented Kingdoms and ephemeral kingships, Attila had the opportunity to be hailed as one of the greatest rulers of the Nomads of Europe. 4. **Continuous geographical expansion:** Because of the non-existence of established national borders, there was scope for limitless geographical expansion.	1. **Unskilled Armed Forces:** Even though the Hunnic Empire was formidable, it was primarily filled with nomadic, uncivilized tribesmen. The advanced negotiation and military capabilities of the Roman Empires would remain a threat all through his reign. 2. **Internal Dissent:** Because of his cruel and barbaric ways, there was always the threat of growing dissent among the survivors of the lands he ravaged. 3. **Non-inclusion:** In his later years, because of his non-inclusiveness and profligacy, he faced the threat of a coup from his own disenchanted followers. 4. **The 2 Roman Empires:** Ever since the first battle with the Eastern European forces on the River Danube, a united attack by the Eastern and Western Roman Empires was always a threat.

WHY IS ATTILA THE HUN A CHARISMATIC LEADER?

A charismatic leader is one who exhumes charm and whose persuasiveness inspires a loyal band of followers. Charismatic leaders are driven by their conviction and dedication to a particular cause. They are very skilled communicators, who are both vocal and emotionally relatable. It is usual for a charismatic leader to take the lead in order to inspire his/her followers to emulate them. The most distinct feature of charismatic leaders is their personality. Their individual personality has a greater influence than anything else in this particular leadership style.

The 5th century A.D. was still a nomadic time in many parts of the world. One of those parts was the Great Hungarian plain. Here there were multiple wandering tribes who had no common language. Their cultures matched to a certain extent. But each staked claim to being stronger than the other, thus, leading to pervasive conflict and division. The annexation by the 2 Roman Empires from the West and South divided them further. Some swore temporary allegiance to the Roman Crowns. Those who didn't, were doomed to suffer at the hands of the repeated incursions by the armed Roman forces. As they were neither armed nor trained to negotiate, they were easy to conquer.

Like any revolutionary movement in history, an inspirational figure motivates the people to undertake collective action. From the beginning, Attila had shown signs of being a committed and dedicated warrior. Together with Bleda, his brother, they had one aim in every battle: to wreak havoc till they were commanded to stop. Their deep seeded hatred for the Romans was also well known and very relatable. The word of their heroic methods soon spread through the Hunnic society. Before they became Kings, they were icons of bravery and fearlessness. Their ascension to the throne as successors to Octar and Rugila was not a matter of discussion. It was inevitable.

While uniting the various tribes of the Central Asia and Eastern Europe, Attila's vision of creating an empire much larger and stronger than the Romans, guided his hand and words. It was more important for him to unite all the tribes (Alans, Gepids, Ostrogoths, Rugians, etc.) by inspiring them to join him on his journey, than to fight them and compel them to submit to his will. Attila's image served him well to secure the loyalty of these tribes (either through dialogue, tribute or simply fear). The Huns united behind him and were the highest ranking warriors in his army. The other tribes were also given prestigious ranks in his army if their exploits of war were worthy of such a reward. Attila made it clear that securing a tribute was a better victory than annihilating the opponent. In this way, they had other Kingdoms and tribes working from their economy while they focussed on capturing territories.

When Attila took the fight to the Eastern Roman Empire, marauding across the Danube River, his image of being the strongest Hun was cemented. The Romans were the foreigners who were partly responsible for the drudgeries of the Hunnic people and the other tribes. They were not welcome across the Danube and the Romans took the liberty to attack their villages whenever they wanted, looting and pillaging settlements. What had been a dream of stomping into Roman territory and decisively crushing their ego became reality because of Attila's daring leadership. Numerous Roman Emperors (Eastern and Western) feared the name of Attila, the Scourge of God. They opened up their cities to Hunnic trade and pledged to pay tonnes of gold to keep him from unleashing his fury on them. Under Attila, the balance of power had shifted and the Huns were the ones being feared. Attila delivered this through fearsome battle techniques, shrewd negotiation and an intimidating reputation. For almost 20 years, a select few would dare cross paths with him.

ATTILA'S DEATH

After the disintegration of his army in the pursuit of Rome, Attila returned to the Great Hungarian Plain with his remaining troops. Attila felt defeated for the first time since he began his life as a conqueror. His image of invincibility had been broken in the eyes of his subjects and worse still, in his own eyes. An uninspired leader is worse than a disenchanted follower. He became less interested in the economics, politics and militaristic decisions of the Hunnic Empire, thus, sowing the seeds for a troubled future.

He sent word of caution to King Marcian that if the tributes were not paid, he could expect a full scale war with the Huns. King Marcian ignored the threat and started spending the gold (meant for Attila's tribute) on building a stronger army to repel future Hunnic attacks.

In 453 A.D., Attila was planning to mount an offensive into Eastern Roman territory. Before he began, Attila settled back into his throne and in the same year, he married a young girl named Ildico, one of his many wives. On the night of their wedding, there was a great feast and debauchery ensued. The next morning, Attila was discovered lifeless. In his drunken stupor, he had suffered a nose bleed and choked to death on his own blood.

ATTILA'S LAST KNOWN LOCATION

After Attila died, there was a period of great mourning amongst his people. Finally, when he was laid to rest, his body, along with many precious stones and burial treasures, was encased in a coffin made of gold. This coffin was put in another coffin made of silver. The second coffin was then put inside an iron coffin. Following this, a dam was built to change the course of a river. Attila's giant encasement was then buried in the riverbed. Once it had been buried, the dam was broken and the river flowed in the same path as before, hiding Attila's burial spot forever.

ATTILA'S KILL COUNT

It is believed that Attila the Hun was responsible for the death of more the 300,000 people (approximately) during his reign. This included men, women and children of a large number of tribes, cities and principalities.

SITUATIONAL LEADERSHIP

WU ZETIAN: CHINA'S SOLE EMPRESS REGENT WHOSE CIRCUMSTANCE DECIDED HER CHARACTER

"The measure of intelligence is the ability to change."

-Albert Einstein

WU ZETIAN
(624 A.D.-705 A.D.)

EMPRESS CONSORT OF THE TANG DYNASTY (655 A.D.-683 A.D.)

GRAND EMPRESS DOWAGER OF THE TANG DYNASTY (683 A.D.-690 A.D.)

EMPRESS REGENT OF THE ZHOU DYNASTY (690 A.D.-705 A.D.)

In the year 654 A.D., Princess Si of Anding was born in the Imperial Chinese household. She was conceived out of wedlock. At this point in time, Emperor Gaozong had become disenchanted by his wife, Empress Wang, and begun distancing himself from her. He was enamoured by another consort of the Imperial household. He was spending more and more time with a high ranking consort named Wu Zetian.

In the imperial Chinese household, it was common for emperors to have multiple consorts who were responsible for different things in the household. For Wu Zetian, this was the second time she had become a member of the Imperial household. During her previous stint, she was a low ranking consort when Emperor Gaozong's father, Emperor Taizong was still alive. She had barely had any contact with the Emperor then. But Wu did have an affair with his son, Li Zhi, who later went on to become the new Emperor of China. During his coronation, he was rechristened as Emperor Gaozong. When his father died, the consorts who had not borne any children to the Emperor were sent away to different temples to continue living as Buddhist nuns. This was a customary practice.

When Wu Zetian had joined the Imperial household, she harboured dreams of one day being a high ranking consort, maybe an Empress if fate smiled upon her kindly. She had left her home and decided to chart a path of her own to rise to prominence. But not everything had gone according to plan. Her dreams had been shattered when she was sent away to live the monastic life in the monastery. She wrote to her previous lover and the new Emperor to rescue her. But the letters did not have any impact on her situation. She served as a nun without any scope to have any earthly desires. Little did she know, this state of hers would be short-lived.

In 650 A.D., a year after Wu Zetian had been living the monastic life, Emperor Gaozong visited the Ganye temple after a thoroughly testing first year as ruler of China. His incompetence as a leader and strategist had become widely known. He had been thoroughly criticized by the public. His tipping point came when he found out that his father had acknowledged his incompetence and had handpicked the brightest and bravest minds of China to serve as his council of advisors. He decided to reassess his situation and seek guidance from Budhha.

Here, the Emperor rediscovered found Wu Zetian. During the visit, he was accompanied by his wife, Empress Consort Wang. She was going through troubles of her own. The Emperor had become enamoured by another consort in the household named Xiao. He had fathered two children with her and was growing distant from his wife. Empress Consort Wang had to turn his attention elsewhere or else he could have replaced her with his new favourite consort. Seeing her husband crying with this nun, she immediately inquired who she was. Upon learning her identity, she saw an opportunity to turn her husband's attention to another woman, till she consolidated a firm hold on her position as the Empress Consort.

She approached Wu Zetian and offered to bring her back to the imperial household. Her instructions to Wu Zetian were to ensure that the Emperor doesn't depose her. Empress Consort Wang's inability to have children had made her insecure and she wanted Wu Zetian to convince her husband of a good future with his present wife. Wu Zetian saw this as an opportunity to permanently return to the Imperial household and restart her unfinished journey. She happily obliged with the Empress' request. She was immediately taken back to the Imperial household.

Reinstating a concubine/consort was considered a grave insult to the previous Emperor that the concubine had served. But Wu Zetian was no ordinary woman. When

Empress Consort Wang suggested this to Emperor Wang, he took extraordinary measures to bring her back to the Imperial household. This included ignoring his advisors and immediate deposition of the highest ranking consort (after Empress Consort Wang) of the household. Wu Zetian was given the title of Zhaoyi, the highest rank among the 9 consorts of second rank.

Soon enough, Emperor Gaozong was no longer enamoured by the Consort Xiao. His attention had firmly turned to Wu Zetian. Within 2 years, they had a boy together named Li Hong. Now, whatever Wu Zetian said acted as direct instructions for the Emperor. The next step for her was to marry the Emperor and be rechristened Empress Consort Wu Zetian. But Empress Consort Wang was still firmly in her place as the wife of the Emperor. For Wu to take the next step in her self-conceived journey of being the ruler of China, she had to become the Empress Consort. To depose Empress Consort Wang, there had to be a very indicting accusation against her.

Princess Si was the second child by Wu Zetian had conceived with the Emperor. Princess Si became famous for a very disturbing reason. One morning, the new born Princess was found lifeless in her cradle. She had been suffocated to death. Wu Zetian was inconsolable. The Emperor was also grieving. In closed quarters, Wu Zetian accused Empress Consort Wang for killing her daughter. She even procured witnesses who testified to Wang's presence near Princess Si's room the night of her death. She also accused Wang's mother of using sorcery to cast spells against her and the Emperor.

The Emperor couldn't see his favourite consort in tears like she was. He immediately deposed Empress Consort Wang. He banished her mother from the Imperial Court. Once they were out of the way, Wu used her immense knowledge of history and past Chinese leaders to advise her husband on official matters. The Emperor was more than happy to have such an able advisor as a close confidant as well. In 655 A.D., Emperor Gaozong married Wu Zetian and her status was elevated to Empress Consort.

This was the first step in the rise of Wu Zetian from a lowly consort in the Imperial to the position of China's one and only female ruler whose reign lasted for almost half a century.

THE IMPERIAL CHINESE EMPIRE BEFORE WU ZETIAN

The Tang dynasty is remembered in Chinese monarchic history as a glorious dynasty that took Chinese civilization to its highest point (known till then) and ushered in a golden age of cosmopolitan culture. Another telling feature of Imperial China at this point in time was its large population. Estimated to have been 80 million strong, the Chinese army was growing to formidable strength under the Tang Dynasty. Along with a strong army, many neighbouring Kingdoms and tribes were paying a large annual tribute to the Chinese Emperor. As a direct consequence of the opulent and giving nature of the Tang Dynasty's rule, the Chinese society believed their Emperor to be wise and powerful. Some even went to the extent of worshipping them like Gods.

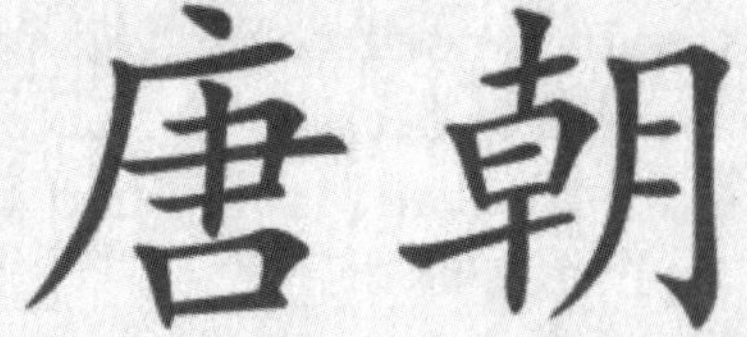

"Tang Dynasty" in Chinese Han characters

Since the fall of the Sui dynasty, the Tangs had been almost unchallenged since they took over in 618 A.D. After the initial years of transition and militaristic succession, Li Shimin, Prince of Qin, began to stake his claim to the throne as early as 621 A.D. After defeating Duo Jiande, the leader of the rebel farmers in the Battle of Hulao where he was heavily outnumbered, Li Shimin achieved legendary status as one who could not only wield many weapons, he was considered a worthy commander as well. After assassinating two of his own elder brothers to ascend to the throne in 626 A.D., his father, Emperor Gaozu of Tang, abdicated and Li Shimin ascended to the throne. As Emperor, he was renamed as Emperor Taizong.

Emperor Taizong of the Tang Dynasty

Emperor Taizong was a ruler of great diplomacy who wasn't afraid to flex his militaristic muscle internationally to prove the might of the Chinese. He was a capable leader who listened to the advice of the wisest members of his council. After the Tang campaign against the Eastern Turks, a Turkic prominent *Khaganate* (army unit of Turks) was destroyed after the capture of its ruler, Illig Qaghan. With this victory, the Turks accepted Emperor Taizong as their *khan* (leader). With this victory, the Chinese grasp on the Asian mainland became firm and unquestioned.

His stories of servitude to the nation were recited, leading to the existence of a 'Personality Cult' amongst majority of the Chinese population. They viewed Taizong as a just and strong leader, who was on a divine mission to establish Chinese dominance across the world. His rule was so impressive that all subsequent rulers and their reign are measured against the achievements of Emperor Taizong and his rule of China.

When Wu Zetian entered the imperial household, it was a place of firm discipline and mature expectation. Even though she believed it was her destiny to have an imperial title one day, that day would not come while she was under the rule of Emperor Taizong. Among other things, the Emperor expected women to adhere to the roles that had been handed down by past generations. Places of political, militaristic and economic discussion had no room for women, not even his own wife. Thus, she continued to work as a lowly consort in the household.

The Emperor's death was fuelled by the constant state of depression that he was in during his later years. This was because of his 2 eldest sons. In 643 A.D., Li Chengqian and Li Tai (the Emperor's eldest sons from his wife, Empress Zhangsun) were fighting a long drawn battle for their ascension to the throne. Even though Li Chengqian was the eldest, Emperor Taizong favoured Li Tai because of his natural ability as a leader. To get Li Tai out of the picture and guarantee his ascension, Li Chengqian plotted an assassination attempt on his father with his most trusted associates and soldiers. But the plot was discovered and the Emperor deposed Li Chengqian. But as he contemplated the situation and discussed the matter with his ministers, he learnt that this assassination attempt had been construed only because of Li Tai initial attempts to dispose of his elder brother with a secret assassination of his own.

The Chinese mainland before the rule of Emperor Taizong of the Tang Dynasty

After numerous exchanges and threats, Emperor Taizong deposed both his eldest sons and sent them into exile where they died soon after. He named his 3rd son (from his wife) as the crown prince and righteous heir to the throne. His name was Li Zhi and he would be renamed Emperor Gaozong. In the closed chambers of the Emperor, the incompetence of Li Zhi (Emperor Gaozong) was being discussed. He was a loner and barely had any influence. He could be scared easily and always relied on others to make his decisions. It was decided that once Li Zhi (Emperor Gaozong) took the throne, he would be surrounded by the most capable military leaders, the wisest chancellors and the most intelligent scholars. This was done to ensure that the world remains unaware of his incompetence.

In 649 A.D., when Emperor Taizong passed away, it was a time of mourning and great sadness. The Chinese empire had lost their most enigmatic and resolute leader. In Emperor Gaozong, China envisioned a similar leader but there was little proof to back it up. In fact, during the first year, there were more rumours about his ineptitude than his ruling ability. His decisions to loosen China's grip on the Korean peninsula and release the Turkic rulers, imprisoned or held under the Tang dynasty, were met with wide criticism. More criticism followed when China was attacked by the same rulers they had released. The country's exemplary reputation as a disciplined and dangerous military force was being swiftly forgotten.

Emperor Gaozong of the Tang Dynasty

During the first year of his rule, Emperor Gaozong was rather depressed and disappointed with how things were going in his empire. He was losing the public's faith. He learnt that he had been considered inept for the position of an Emperor by his own father and the popular opinion was that if it hadn't been for the folly of his two elder brothers, he did not deserve to ascend to the throne. There was also proof that his father had considered another son of his (from a consort named Yang) for the post of Emperor, but refrained from doing so as per the advice of his close aides. These matters were now public information and the public had many things to say about their Emperor. Gaozong was not a born leader and it was becoming increasingly likely that he could not be guided to be one either.

WU ZETIAN'S RISE TO POWER AND SUBSEQUENT RULE

MISSION: To re-establish the Zhou Dynasty in China with a reputation of enviable militaristic might, resolute diplomatic policies and a progressive society for all members of the Chinese Empire.

A concubine, by definition, is a woman who lives with a married man but has a lower status than his wife. This is a prominent feature of polygamous societies, especially among the Emperors of Imperial China. In the Emperor's household, the concubines were called consorts and were given ranks based on skill and experience. Even though the word "Empress" did not exist in the language spoken in China during imperial times, the wife of the Emperor was considered higher than all the concubines and they would refer to her as "Empress Consort". All concubines were given one of 9 ranks or their associated sub ranks and household jobs. Regardless of rank, it was standard practice for the Emperor to have sexual relations with his concubines. In fact, many Emperors had chosen their heirs from the children conceived with one of his many concubines.

In 638 A.D., the Tang Dynasty had been ruling China for 20 years. Emperor Taizong was an able ruler who commanded respect for his diplomatic and militaristic abilities. One of his official concubines had vacated her post. She was a low ranked consort and the Empress Consort ordered for a suitable successor to be found.

Titles in the Imperial household	Rank
Empress (皇后; *huáng hòu*)	1
Consort (夫人 *furen*)	2 (sub ranking from 1-4 for selected concubines)
Nine Concubines (九嬪 *jiupin*)	3 (sub-ranking from 1-9 for selected concubines)
Handsome Fairness (婕妤 *jieyu*)	4
Beauty (美人 *meiren*)	5
Talented (才人 *cairen*)	6
Lady of Treasure (寶林 *baolin*)	7
Lady of His Majesty (御女 *yunü*)	8
Selected Lady (采女 a*cainü*)	9

Wu Zetian was the daughter of Wu Shihuo, the Governor of 3 districts in the Jiangling County in Hebei (Yangzhou, Lizhou and Jingzhou). He was a progressive man who had insisted on his daughter being educated and instilled a literary inclination in her. She had been raised in a home with many servants. She was not well versed with household chores or the management of it. In fact, she had been raised in an environment where she was served and cared for. Much like a princess or a queen. She was also trained in the manners and practices associated with the imperial class, by both her mother and father.

When her father was informed of the opportunity, he immediately recommended his daughter to fill the position of the Emperor's new concubine. The Empress Consort was impressed with her refined presence and outstanding knowledge of literature. She was happy to accept Wu Zetian and sent instruction for her to join the Emperor's household as soon as possible.

Illustration of the Imperial Palace in Olfert Dapper's Memorable Bedryf

In Imperial China, once a woman had been inducted into the imperial household as a concubine, she could not return to her parent's home. She could only visit them, infrequently. It was not a compulsion, but a practice that had come to be widely accepted over time. The other accepted norm was that "once a concubine, always a concubine". That is, most concubines would never see the Emperor, apart from when he requested their presence himself. This would seldom happen. The only time their presence would be requested by the Emperor was when he wanted to engage in sexual intercourse with them. As a result, it was widely believed that there was almost no hope for a concubine to rise to a position of power or influence.

The rank chosen for Wu Zetian was that of *Cairen* or the "talented" concubine. She was given the role of a type of secretary. In this role, she kept studying literature along with her role as a junior administrator. She was expected to keep to herself and not be seen by the Emperor. Her job was simply to manage the day-to-day workings of a certain part of the household and to spend the rest of her time in her small chamber.

Emperor Taizong was a man of strong principle and a sense of devout servitude. It is believed that even though he had respect for Wu Zetian, he never actually engaged in an extra-marital affair with her. But the same cannot be said about his youngest son. Li Zhi, who would later go on to be Emperor Gaozong of Tang, was infatuated by his father's young consort. Even though it was frowned upon, Li Zhi had an affair with her while she was still serving his father. But as the days passed, the affair ended and Wu Zetian was reminded of her place as a lowly consort among the higher ranked ladies of the household.

After Emperor Taizong passed away, Wu Zetian's time in the Imperial household was temporarily ended. It was customary for the Emperor's consorts, who had not conceived children with the Emperor, to embrace a life of celibacy and live as nuns in a Buddhist monastery. Wu Zetian was consigned to the Ganye Buddhist temple with the same expectation. But she was not ready to embrace this life. In an attempt to escape it, she wrote to the new Emperor, her former lover. She requested to be enlisted in his household as a concubine because the monastic life did not even allow her

The typical look of a Buddhist Nun

the basic pleasure of reading and reciting prose. She sought the life that she had been blessed with for almost a decade in the company of Chinese royalty. But, at that time, her plea had fallen on deaf ears. Wu Zetian had reluctantly accepted her fate, shaved her hair and began to settle into life as a nun.

However, within a year, someone came for her. The person who came to rescue her from the monastery, however, would not be the new Emperor. It was his wife, Empress Consort Wang.

Emperor Gaozong was married to the crown princess Wang. When he ascended to the throne, crown princess Wang was re-titled Empress Consort Wang. But their marriage had been fraught with trouble right from the start. Because of an unidentified reason, Empress Wang could not have children and the young Emperor had turned to a concubine named Xiao to fulfil his need for an heir. As time passed, he grew closer to Xiao, fathering 3 children with her. Because of Gaozong's impulsive and naïve decision making history, Empress Consort Wang felt that because of her inability to conceive, he may replace her soon and it would not be an uncommon occurrence. She had to find a solution.

POLITICAL CLIMATE OF IMPERIAL CHINA

Political State: Imperialist state, ruled by the Emperor/Empress in a male dominated society

Geographic Division: The Chinese empire extended from Korean Peninsula up to Central Asia, almost till modern day Kashmir in India

Land Ownership: China was one of the first countries to implement written laws (with sub-articles). In the past, because of ease of forgery, the country suffered from numerous cases of documentation forgery

Relatively Transparent Selection System: Written examinations were conducted for all important government posts, followed by an interview at the Imperial palace.

During a thoroughly testing first year, in 650 A.D., Emperor Gaozong once decided to pray and hope for guidance from Lord Buddha. The Emperor and his wife visited the famed Ganye Temple. There, he lit candles all over the temple. He sat in quiet contemplation and meditated. When he opened his eyes, he saw a familiar face. It was Wu Zetian. She had no hair and wore a simple white cloth. The young Emperor, upon seeing her face, began to weep. She had been locked away in the monastery and the face of a man she had been intimate with triggered an emotional response from Wu Zetian too. She too wept.

Seeing this, Empress Wang approached Wu Zetian and asked her to return to the Imperial household under her instruction. Wu Zetian asked why she wanted her, a woman her husband had an affair with, to return to their household. Empress Wang confided in her that her husband had become enamoured by another woman named Xiao in the household. She told Wu Zetian that she felt her position as the Empress Consort was under threat and she needed her to distract the Emperor from the consort Xiao. The Empress promised her the freedom to read as much as she wanted. But her duty was to whisper to the Emperor to keep Empress Consort Wang in her position.

650 A.D.-683 A.D.: The Rise of the New Empress Consort Wu Zetian

Reinstating a concubine who had served the Emperor's father was considered highly inappropriate. But in 650 A.D., Emperor Gaozong was willing to accept the criticism and reinstated her on the recommendation of his wife. Wu Zetian was given the title of *Zhaoyi* (the highest rank among the 9 concubines of second rank in the hierarchy) and was referred to as Consort Wu. Soon, their romantic affair was reignited and by 653 A.D., Wu had conceived two boys with the Emperor, Li Hong and Li Xian. Much like Consort Xiao, Consort Wu was now the young Emperor's favourite. Soon, Xiao and Wang combined forces to remove Consort Wu from the position of power that she had gained. But it was to no avail. And in the year 654 A.D., Consort Wu began to pave the way for her ascension to the highest rank in the Imperial household.

Consort Wu had given birth to a daughter, fathered by the Emperor. But the baby soon died. The medical examiner concluded the child had died due to asphyxiation. Wu accused Empress Wang of strangulating and killing her daughter. She even arranged witnesses to testify to seeing Empress Wang near the child's room on the night of the supposed murder. The Emperor was sympathetic to Consort Wu and became adamant to remove Empress Wang as the Empress Consort. It was speculated that Wu asphyxiated her own daughter in order to make this elaborate plot to depose Empress Wang.

Tension had begun in the Imperial household and in the summer of 655 A.D. Wu again accused Empress Wang and her mother, Lady Liu, of using witchcraft. Summarily, Lady Liu was admonished and banned from the Imperial court. Wang's father was demoted and a council was assembled to discuss the fate of the Empress. By now, a large portion of the assembly had pledged their allegiance to the enigmatic new Consort who seemed knowledgeable, wise and appropriately cunning. Although no clear majority was established at the end of the meeting, Emperor Gaozong placed Empress Wang under arrest and in 655 A.D. He married Consort Wu. Her title was now changed to Empress Consort Wu.

ECONOMIC PROFILE OF IMPERIAL CHINA

Primary Work: Grain farming and cloth production

Taxation System: All agricultural produce was taxed to support the armed forces of China

Agrarian Economy: On the Chinese mainland, there was a large area of sanctioned cultivable land to create a self-sufficient agrarian economy.

Fubing System: The Fubing system ensured militiamen could support themselves by farming on the land the Empress provided them. The soldiers worked on their land (with/without subsistence farmers) throughout peak farming seasons, and then were given military training during the off-seasons

The Silk Road: China reopened the Silk Road, the world's largest land-based trade route, under the command of Empress Wu. As a result, foreign trade once again flourished in China

Trading Currency: Chinese Coin

In 656 A.D., Li Zhong (Gaozong's eldest son from a concubine named Liu) was deposed from being his heir apparent and Empress Consort Wu's son with the Emperor, Li Hong, was made the crown prince and the heir apparent. The time had come for Wu to establish her prominence and she ordered the execution or exile of all those who had opposed her including chancellor Zhangsun Wuji, who had served Emperor Gaozong and his father before him. After this purge, there was no official who would dare raise a doubt or a question against the Emperor or the Empress Consort.

By 660 A.D., Li Zhong, former heir apparent was also targeted and placed under house arrest. She was essentially wiping out all opposition to her impending reign. The only person who would stand in the way of her ascension to a position of supreme power would be her husband, Emperor Gaozong. The same year, the Emperor started suffering from painful headaches and partial loss of vision. It was rumoured that she was slowly poisoning the Emperor but no one could point a finger at her without facing the risk of execution. The Emperor was getting increasingly incapacitated and he installed Empress Consort Wu in his place to rule on the petitions from the various officials and officers. Because of rich knowledge of culture and history, she made rulings that were seen as ones that would make China stronger internally.

By 664 A.D., she was rivalling the authority of the Emperor.

IMPERIAL CHINA'S SOCIAL NORMS

Living Status: Settled society with many districts and prefectures

Major Religion(s): Buddhism along with a minority following of Taoism

Language: Middle Chinese

Common Practices:

a) Calligraphy was a popular skill as it would help secure a job in the government.

b) Meritocracy was promoted to recruit the most able candidates for government jobs

c) Fishing and animal slaughter was banned as Empress Wu was considered the "Maitreya Buddha" and under her instruction, consumption of meat was not acceptable

Education: Many public schools were opened to increase literacy and promote a reading habit among the general population

This made Emperor Gaozong sceptical and insecure. He began to question her motives, especially after she supposedly enlisted Taoist sorcerer Guo Xingzhen to use witchcraft. When he confronted her about this, she pleaded her case and called it propaganda by the former Empress Wang. She further called it a plot by the former empress and his heir apparent Li Zhong to weaken their bond. Emperor couldn't bear to see his Empress Consort in tears. He immediately ordered the execution of the conspirators, including his former wife and forced his own son, Li Zhong, to commit suicide while under house arrest. Since then, the duo of the Emperor Gaozong and Empress Consort Wu became known as the "Two Holy Ones" in the Imperial court.

Empress Consort Wu spent the next 10 years establishing her family in the Imperial order with many of her relatives being given titles of "Prince", "Princess", "Duke" and "Duchess". Even within her family, she purged those who would oppose, question or challenge her authority. By 675 A.D., Emperor Gaozong was sufficiently ill for the Empress Consort to be considered the proxy ruler of China. Her own son, heir apparent and crown prince Li Hong, died suddenly that year under rather sketchy circumstances. In 680 A.D., her other son from the Emperor, Li Xian was also deposed and exiled. His younger brother, Li Zhe, was then installed as the crown prince and heir apparent. In 683 A.D., Emperor Gaozong died in his castle in Luoyang. Li Zhe took the throne as Emperor Zhingzong. Soon, it became clear that he was only a puppet Emperor (much like his father) whose strings were being pulled by his mother. Empress Consort Wu's title had been renewed to Empress Dowager.

During this period of 30 years, controversially dubbed as "Gaozong reign", China lost many territories. The Silk Road had been shut. Indigenous trade was suffering. Trade relations with neighbouring Kingdoms and nations had suffered. Internal politics had become focussed on the relationship between the Emperor and his wife. The country suffered droughts and many outlying provinces had been so neglected that they had withered away. In comparison to his father's legendary reign, Emperor Gaozong's reign was characterized by loss of stature, economic recession and political in-fighting.

683 A.D.-690 A.D.: The Grand Empress Dowager Wu

Empress Consort Wu was now called Empress Dowager as the widow of late Emperor Gaozong. The new Emperor was her third son, Li Zhe. In his will, Emperor Gaozong had left instruction that Empress Dowager Wu had to be consulted on all major decisions, whether military or civil. Upon ascending to the throne, Li Zhe took the name Emperor Zhongzong. But his reign would be rather short lived.

From the first day, Emperor Zhongzong showed signs of resisting Empress Dowager Wu's instructions. His wife, Empress Wei, wanted to follow in the footsteps of her mother-in-law and exercise control over imperial matters. She had her father appointed China's prime minister. Chancellor Pei Yan informed Empress Dowager Wu of this and she was not happy. She deposed Emperor Zhongzong (six weeks after his appointment). She had his father-in-law accused of treason and sent into complete seclusion. She had her youngest son, Li Dan, installed as the new Emperor. He took the name Emperor Ruizong. But that was only a front for her rule.

In the court, she no longer sat behind the curtain. She sat in front of the court and her son's decisions were made by her. She appointed a secret police to monitor those who were contemplating rising up against her. The secret police were known to have written a document called the Manual of Accusation, which detailed steps for interrogation and obtaining confessions by torture. One of these methods, the "Dying Swine's Melancholy", was one in which the victim had their limbs and tongue amputated, then force-fed and left to wallow in their own excrement. Word about their brutality spread quickly and a culture of reporting on conspirers against the Empress Dowager Wu became common practice. Copper mailboxes were placed outside the Imperial residence for citizens to report on those who opposed her. Soon, the rebellions and protests were no longer on the streets. The matter had become one that only the powerful and entitled could take up. Thus, she had quelled the resistance once again. Emperor Ruizong had no authority or control in Imperial matters. As a sign of protest, he refused to move to the Imperial Palace.

IMPERIAL CHINA'S TECHNOLOGY ADVANCES

Materials: Metals like iron, steel and copper were being manufactured

Main Weapons: Bow/arrow, steel swords (Jian and Dao), long spears, cannons and chinese axe (Fu)

Inventions: There were many inventions and discoveries in different fields during the reign of Empress Wu, primarily due to her decision to reopen the Silk Road:

Fields:

a) Timekeeping

b) Mechanical and structural engineering

c) Medicine

d) Alchemy

Inventions:

a) Playing cards

b) Mass woodblock printing

Communication Systems: Courier system of message delivery

In 686 A.D., even though Emperor Ruizong was the righteous ruling Emperor, Empress Dowager Wu offered him the chance to take his rightful place next to her in the Imperial court. But he refused as he would only be a puppet. In 688 A.D., the greatest purge of all was initiated. Under the guise of offering sacrifices in the Luo River on the death anniversary of her late husband, she invited all the senior members of the Tang dynasty's imperial Li clan. Believing that they were being invited to their own execution, they chose to rise up against her. But before they could plan a coordinated attack, Empress Dowager Wu's troops got wind of their plans. They executed or arrested almost every member of the Li clan across China. This included all the Princes and the granduncles of her late husband. They were either forced to commit suicide, starved to death or executed. By 690 A.D., she purged the Li clan (the bloodline of Emperor Taizong and Gaozong) and only far reaching relatives would remain who had no real claim to the throne.

690 A.D.-705 A.D.: Empress Regent Wu Zhao and the Zhou Dynasty

On October 16th, 690 A.D., Empress Dowager Wu climbed the stairs of the imperial court for the last time as one who could be considered second only to the Emperor. She sat in her throne and was crowned the Empress Regent of the Imperial Kingdom of China. She would no longer need a man to represent her or speak for her in front of the Imperial court. Her word was final now. She renamed the Tang Dynasty to the Zhou Dynasty and forced many of her own offspring to abandon the "Li" name (a standard surname of the Tang Dynasty) for the name of the new dynasty she would install. This marked the beginning of the relatively short lived reign of the Zhou dynasty under Wu Zetian or as she was later called, Empress Regent Wu Zhao.

An illustration of the Maitreya Buddha

Even though she was Empress Regent, there were many who considered her reign a gross bastardization of the Imperial code. In the initial years, she ruled with an iron fist to dispel these notions and rumours about her. Those who rebelled were harshly put down. Those who conspired against her were summarily executed or exiled. This included generals, officers and citizens. She took a hard look at the country's economic and military matters. She wanted China's reputation as a strong military force to be reinstated as soon as possible.

As her first move, she recast the Nine Tripod Cauldrons, the symbol of ultimate power in Ancient China, to establish her supremacy and reinforce her authority. She had a note about the "Great Cloud Sutra" distributed among the people that spoke about the coming of the Maitreya Buddha, the female from of the Buddha who would reform all that is wrong in society. Because of this, she reinvented her image as the "All Caring Mother" of the Chinese people. One of her first reforms was increasing the cultivable land area in the country. This led to an increase in the number of farming households from 3.8 million to 6.2 million. Along with this, she kept taxes low and made sure there was periodic reallocation of land to protect the status of free and self-standing peasants. Because of the equitable distribution of land and subsequent wealth, the general populace felt loved by the new "Maitreya Buddha".

Apart from just improving the land allocation, she also brought about changes in the system of selection of government employees and officers. Under her rule, the number of schools also increased. This was to train more people for the role of government officials. She also instituted a public examination system to appoint worthy candidates to become office bearers. This was to effectively expunge the system of aristocracy-based appointment of government officers. Apart from the initial appointment, all government officers were required to take a periodic examination called *keju* to evaluate an officer's capability and knowledge base. Following the examination, there would be a final interview in the Imperial court so the best could be selected for the important positions.

Empress Regent Wu also led China to reclaim territories in Tibet which were lost under the reign of Emperor Taizong. After the initial battles, it was clear that a rebuilding exercise was needed. She demoted the commanders Wang Xiaojie and Lou Shide because of their ineptitude to repel the attacks

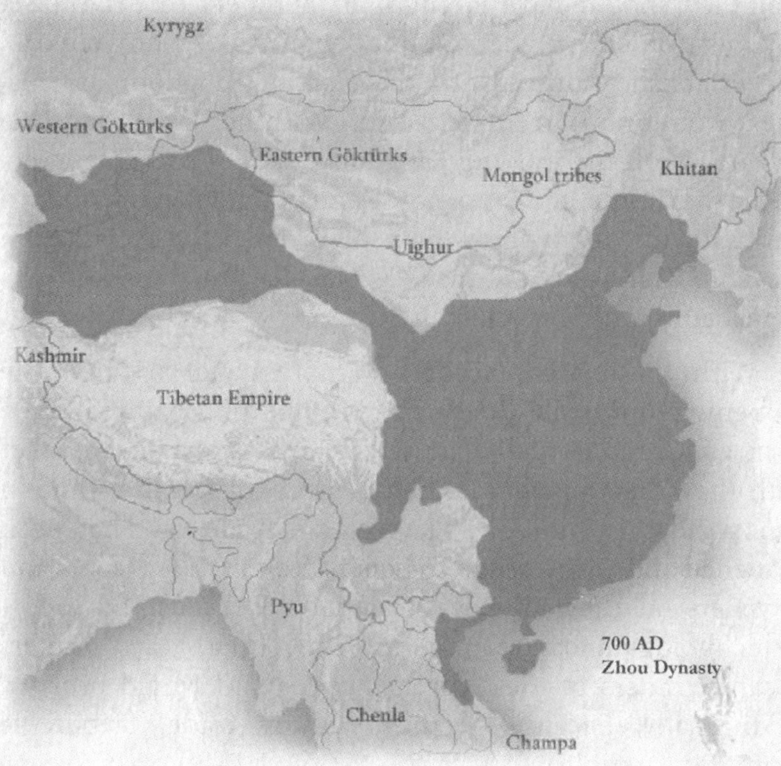

The Chinese Empire under the rule of Empress Wu Zhou

from the Tibetan General Gar Tringring Tsendro. Because of these losses, she had to negotiate a tough treaty of peace with the Tibetans which included the return of the prisoners of war and paying an annual tribute to Ashina Muchou, the Khan of the Tibetan populace, which included seeds, silk, tools and iron.

The Empress Regent urged men of all ages of her country to join the armed forces and offered land in return for their service. In addition to serving the nation, they would also do their families a service by giving them cultivable land. Soon, many young and able men began to join the army in large numbers. If the leadership of the army would not be capable enough to deal with foreign threats, the Empress believed that they should have strength in numbers to drive back any invasion and further, mount conquests of many regions. She established peace with the Korean Kingdom of Silla, but it would not last for very long. With her large army, she defeated both the warring Kingdoms of Silla and Goguryeo. At the same time, she oversaw the end of the Tibetan-Western Turk alliance, following which she ordered the reclamation the Four Garrisons of Anxi (Kucha, Khotan, Kashgar and Karashahr), which was lost in 668 A.D.

With these areas secured, Empress Wu ordered the reopening of the Silk Road. This brought international trade back to China, which had seized ever since the conflict with the Tibetan Khanates had begun. For the first time in almost 70 years, the world's largest land trade route had been reopened and China stood to benefit from it. The traders and travellers on the Silk Road brought unprecedented inflow of technology and foreign goods into China. Many farmers became traders of these foreign goods and would prosper. Additionally, because of the resulting trade, favourable terms were established with the Middle East for many years. Empress Wu was hailed for this decision and was celebrated in her later years for bringing globalization to China.

Empress Regent Wu was widely considered a saviour for the Chinese people bringing education, meritocracy and foreign trade back into the identity of China. Conversely, there were still many rumours about her supposed favouritism towards those who massaged her ego and satisfy her supposed "insatiable" sexual appetite. There were rebellions threatening her reign, but despite these rumours and uprisings, she continued to rule the country with the intention of making China the greatest economic and militaristic power in the world. In 705 A.D., a palace coup forced her to abdicate and move out of the Imperial palace.

STRENGTH-WEAKNESS-OPPORTUNITY-THREAT (SWOT) ANALYSIS OF WU ZETIAN

STRENGTHS	WEAKNESSES
1. **"Empress Wu":** Wu Zetian created the word Empress, devoid of the title of Consort. She had the word created in their spoken language to honour herself as the first and only female ruler of Imperial China. 2. **Adamant:** During her tenure and after abdication, Wu Zetian had always been adamant about her beliefs and methods. Even though she had been given many accusatory and derogatory titles, she was never deterred and continued on her path. 3. **Diplomatic:** In an age where one's influence could be easily undermined because of her gender, Wu Zetian ruled with appropriate diplomacy in matter of economic and political importance. 4. **Good Listener:** Because of her skills as a listener, she was able to navigate her way through most of her obstacles and stop those who opposed her.	1. **Overtly Meticulous:** This flaw of hers led to her losing many of her followers after the peak of her rule. Her need to control how people perceived her would be the distraction that led to her eventual abdication. 2. **Superstitious:** Even though she was well-read, Wu Zetian was still superstitious and took many natural happenings as signs of her downfall. It is said that she believed the spirits of Consorts Xiao and Empress Wang haunted her throughout her life. 3. **Obstinate:** After she came to power, her obstinate behaviour disenchanted her court and followers who eventually would use it to force her abdication.
OPPORTUNITIES	**THREATS**
1. **Reopened the Silk Road:** After a series of plagues and disputes along the internationally renowned trade road, it was reopened under the command of Empress Wu. This connected China to the West for land-based trade. This allowed global influence to exist in Chinese markets and culture. 2. **Consolidated Chinese rule in the Korean peninsula:** The Korean peninsula had been secured in 675 and the Empress Consort Wu made it clear that the peninsula must stay under their control and hub for Chinese influence. 3. **Practiced tolerance and social equality:** Throughout her reign, Empress Wu was highly regarded in the general populace for her inclination towards promoting the literary, expressive and performance arts in society. Apart from this, she also promoted the existence of multiple religions and the practice of judging people by merit, not lineage. 4. **The Great Cloud Sutra:** According to Buddhist texts, it was said that the revolution would be brought by rise of a female leader in the Chinese society. Empress Wu used this, the Great Cloud Sutra, as a mass propaganda tool and her acceptance of many social changes served to reinforce and enhance her reputation as the saviour of the people.	1. **Recurring threat from the followers of the Tang Dynasty:** When she renamed the dynasty as the Zhou Dynasty, it caused outrage among the conservatives and traditionalists in the Chinese society. Empress Wu, during her reign, had repeatedly been threatened with uprisings and assassinations by those loyal to the Tang Dynasty. 2. **Gender Politics:** As China had never had a female ruler before, it was a cause of great debate among the ruling class whether they should follow the word of a woman. Even though she quelled the rebellions, there was always the threat of some sort of ill-conceived action from her detractors.

WHY WU ZETIAN IS THE EPITOME OF SITUATIONAL LEADERSHIP?

Situational leadership is one in which there is no fixed type of leadership. In fact, this leadership is characterized by its ability to change as per the situation. A situational leader adapts to the situation and influences his/her followers to do the same. The most effective leaders are those that are able to adapt their style to the situation and look at visible cues to get the job done. The right style of leadership depends greatly on the maturity level (i.e., the level of knowledge and competence) of the followers. The situational approach to leadership also avoids the pitfalls of the single-style approach by recognizing that there are many different ways of dealing with a problem and that leaders need to be able to assess a situation in order to determine what approach will be the most effective at any given moment.

Wu Zetian's Children:

1. Li Hong

- 652 A.D. - 675 A.D.
- Cause of death: Supposedly murdered by Wu Zetian

2. Princess Si of Anding

- 654 A.D. - 654 A.D.
- Cause of Death: Supposedly murdered by Wu Zetian

3. Li Xian

- 655 A.D. – 684 A.D.
- Cause of Death: Forced to commit suicide by Wu Zetian

4. Li Xian aka Emperor Zhongzong

- 656 A.D. – 710 A.D.
- Cause of Death: Supposedly poisoned by his wife Empress Wei

5. Li Dan aka Emperor Ruizong

- 662 A.D. – 716 A.D.
- Cause of Death: Natural causes

6. Li Lingyue (disputed) aka Princess Taiping

- 665 A.D. – 713 A.D.
- Cause of Death: Forced to commit suicide

Wu Zetian, aka Empress Consort Wu, aka Empress Dowager Wu, aka Empress Regent Wu, did what few leaders do in their formative years. She read extensively. She learnt the leadership methods of great rulers of the past. She learnt the ways of societies. The final result of this method-based, situational approach was the realization of her vision to be the first female Empress Regent of China.

There were many faces of Wu Zetian, each unique to those who were involved in a particular realm of her life. She was benevolent to the masses, ruthless to those seeking favour because of lineage, intelligent to the ruling class, a visionary to those involved in arts and literature, and a vile opportunist to the tradionalists. In essence, her style was one fuelled by adaptation to situation and circumstance. Her ability allowed Wu Zetian to take different roles during her life and no one, not even her closest aides, would generally be aware of her next move or what she was thinking.

EMPRESS REGENT WU ZHAO'S DEATH

By spring 705 A.D., Empress Regent Wu Zetian had become gravely ill. She had become delirious and was known to have made some ill-conceived decisions at the time about her immediate advisors. This is attributed to the influence exerted on her by the Zhang brothers, her supposed lovers who would whisper to her during times of intimacy. They wanted her to leave the empire to them upon her death. Both brothers were killed in a palace coup that resulted in the forced abdication of Empress Regent Wu. She agreed to vacate Changsheng hall (her residence) and was moved to a subsidiary palace called Shangyang Palace.

Over the next months, her health deteriorated further and she became more or less silent. On 16th December, 705 A.D., she died in her bed. In the last edict issued by her, she refused to be addressed as Empress Regent Wu Zetian anymore. Instead, she wanted to be addressed as Empress Consort Zetian Dasheng.

EMPRESS CONSORT ZETIAN DASHENG'S LAST KNOWN LOCATION

She was buried next to her husband, Emperor Gaozong, at the the Qianling Mausoleum, near the then-capital city of Chang'an, on Mount Liang. Her tombstone reads "Empress Consort Zetian Dasheng".

EMPRESS CONSORT ZETIAN DASHENG'S KILL COUNT

Empress Consort Wu Zetian aka Grand Empress Dowager Wu Zetian aka Empress Regent Wu Zhao aka Empress Consort Zetian Dahseng had killed many people during her reign. While there is no official figures on how many people killed, directly and indirectly, she was responsible for the suppression of the Li Clan of the Tang Dynasty; multiple chancellors; purging of countless government officers and generals; families who spoke against her; scholars and intellectuals who opposed her rule; protestors and soldiers by sending them for suicide missions against the Turkish and Tibetan Khanates, between 650 A.D. to 705 A.D. This included men, women and children, including the debatable asphyxiation of her infant daughter and the slow execution of her 2 sons while they were in exile.

TEMUJIN BORJIGIN a.k.a. GENGHIS KHAN
(1162 A.D. – 1227 A.D.)

KHAN OF THE MONGOLS (1186 A.D.–1187 A.D.)

'KHAGAN' (KING OF KINGS) OF THE UNITED MONGOL EMPIRE (1206 A.D. – 1227 A.D.)

In 1162 A.D., in the mountains of Northern Mongolia, a woman screamed in pain. She was about to give birth. She was burning up from a fever and her cries could be heard throughout the village. The mid-wives and caregivers arranged everything for her. The woman was the wife of the chief of the Khamag Mongol tribe. Her name was Hoelun. Her husband, Yesugei, was waiting for his wife to deliver as he sat with his general and guards in a hut, far away from her. Their tribe name was Borjigin.

The women with Hoelun tried to calm her down and urged to push harder. And so she did. She was a strong woman but this was the first time she was giving birth. She had not known this pain before. But she believed in a lesson, one that she would teach her son in her later years, "No job is complete till it is finished". So she persisted and kept pushing. Soon, he came screaming to life. A healthy baby boy. Eyes closed, he emerged from his mother's womb with a blood clot clasped in his fist. All the ladies in the hut gasped. They proceeded to clean her up and the little boy. But he would not let go of the clot in his hand. He had ripped it from his mother's womb on his way out of her.

In Mongol myth, it was said that he who was born holding a blood clot in his hand was destined to be a great ruler. Maybe even the greatest. The ladies covered the infant with a cloth and cradled him in their arms. Each took turns looking at the delicate boy, speaking in tongues wishing for his good health and long life. Finally, when Hoelun was conscious again, they put her new born son in her arms. She held him close and gently bounced him. Her little protector was here. She told one of the women in the tent to bring her husband in to the tent to see his first born. Yesugei rushed to the tent and was welcomed with a smile on his wife's tired face. His son stared up at him with a witless expression.

Yesugei had worked long and hard to form the first confederation of Mongol tribes. In his conquest, he had fought battles with many tribes and formed favourable alliances with many of them to form a united confederation. It was the most favourable way to build a strong contiguous empire. The most recent of his captives was a Tatar chief named Temujin-uge. But he had no intention of torturing or killing his most recent prisoner, even the Tatars were the sworn enemies of the Khagan Mongols. He wanted to negotiate a favourable truce between the Tatar and the Khamag Mongol confederation, thus ending decades of fighting and killing.

As a tribute to his prisoner, Yesugei suggested to Hoelun that they name their first born Temujin. Before she agreed, Hoelun told him that he had come out from her, grasping a blood clot. Yesugei took a moment for the importance of that incident seep in. Yesugei wanted his son to follow in his footsteps. By naming the boy after another ruler would be a good lesson about benevolence and diplomacy. Both parents agreed on the name and he was christened Temujin Borjigin.

Any prophesy ever conjured, always makes a statement without any detail whatsoever. It is in the details that the real truth is embedded. Temujin's early years were riddled with poverty and forced servitude. His marriage was arranged at the age of 9 to a girl named Borte of the tribe Khongirad. He was to be officially married when he was 12 years old. This was just the start.

Temujin's father was poisoned by the same Tatars with whom Yesugei had attempted to form an alliance. When he laid claim to his father's throne as the eldest son, his claim was rejected unanimously. He was cast away by the Khagan Mongols and his family was abandoned. His wife had to remain with her tribe. For many years after that, Temujin, his siblings (including his half-brothers) and his mother lived as scavengers. They ate wild fruits and carcasses of oxen and small animals. Till this point, the prophecy foretold for Temujin seemed like a soothsayer's lie. Temujin was timid and focussed on his hunting and scavenging skills.

In the wilderness, the family slowly began losing their integrity. Temujin's elder half-brother Begter (not born of Hoelun) began to exercise his authority as the eldest of the family and wanted to take Hoelun as his wife. He wanted to do this to become the leader of the family. Not only would this be an incestuous insult, but it would desecrate the honour of his mother, whom he deeply loved and respected. Temujin's anger had been stoked and for the first time, his rage began to guide his hand. His younger brother Khasar told Temujin that he too strongly opposed Begter's claim on their mother. Soon after, on a hunting excursion, Khasar spoke to Begter and tried to change his decision. Begter had become adamant and dismissed Khasar's suggestion. Upon hearing this, Temujin erupted with an ungodly rage and slaughtered his eldest half-brother.

When they returned, Temujin confessed to Hoelun what he had done. In that moment, her reaction to this confession would mould the man her son would become. She supported his actions, hailed him as the male head of their family and declared that they would follow Temujin's instructions as their decree. Temujin was 14 years old.

By 1177 A.D., at 15 years of age, he began to bring together other nomads to conduct raids on any and every tribe they would come across. He was not yet idolized, but he was slowly building a reputation of being a ruthless and relentless warrior. He was captured numerous times by his father's former allies and enemies. Temujin, from a young age, had developed a persuasive way of speaking to compliment his daring escape attempts. While escaping from captivity during his early years, he found those who would remain loyal to him till the end of his reign. While escaping captivity from the Tayichi'ud, Temujin met Jelme, Bo'orchu and Chiluan, all of whom would serve as his generals during his rise to power.

The same year, Temujin had established his home next to the Senggür river. His home was a portable hut (called yurt) which was the standard housing for Mongols. Then, he went to his father-in-law and asked for his wife to be returned to him. After he gave a fine black sable jacket as dowry, Borte returned to her husband. But within a few days, their yurt was attacked by Merkits, the sworn enemy of the Khagan Mongols. Borte was kidnapped and held in captivity of 8 months.

Temujin plotted his revenge. He would need a small army to retrieve her and inflict significant damage on the Merkits for dishonouring him and his family. He reached out to a Khan named Toghrul, the ruler of the Keraites tribe. Toghrul was anda (sworn blood brother) to Temujin's father. His proposal to the Toghrul was that his wife Borte had been captured by the Merkits tribe and he sought to bring her back. Toghrul, in the honour of Temujin's father and impressed by his respectful demeanour, granted him 20,000 of his warriors.

Toghrul made him aware of another Khan who was growing in power and one who knew Temujin personally. He instructed Temujin to align himself to him. Jamukha, Temujin's anda (blood brother), had grown in power and prominence in his own tribe. After his family had been abandoned by the tribe, Jamukha too had left the Khagan Mongols. Jamukha had faced many struggles in his ascension to power as well. When Temujin approached headstrong Jamukha, old blood brothers were reunited. They won the battle decisively and Temujin's wife Borte returned to him.

By 1186 A.D., there were whispers in the Khagan Mongol tribe that Temujin is the great Khan who would lead all the Mongols owing to his intelligent and belligerent attitude. He was also heavily supported by Toghrul. Jamukha himself had consolidated powerful and was heavily favoured too. But Jamukha believed that there is no room for two rulers of the growing Mongol Empire, just like there cannot be 2 suns in the sky. In addition, their beliefs were starkly opposite. Through years of hardship, Temujin had learnt the effectiveness of rewarding loyalty and meritocracy. Jamukha, on the other hand, believed in Mongolian aristocracy and following lineage. This difference between the two blood brothers led to rising tensions within their camps.

During a congregation attended by both of them, a shaman named Kokochu claimed Temujin to be the great Khan who was destined to rule the world. This did not help improve relations between the two blood brothers. The same year, supported by Toghrul, Temujin was elected Khan of the Mongols.

Jamukha was outraged. Immediately after the election, he, with 30,000 troops, attacked Temujin in 1187 A.D. This battle was called the Battle of Dalan Balzhut. Temujin acted swiftly to build a defence, but it could not be done in time. In his first battle as ruler of the Mongols, he was easily and completely defeated. In the aftermath, Toghrul was exiled and Jamukha laid claim to the title of the Great Khan of all Mongols. While everyone knew Jamukha to be an able ruler, his first action shocked many into fleeing or submission. He ordered his troops to collect the followers of Temujin who were still alive (about 70 of them), and in front of everyone, boiled them alive in cauldrons. Even his own soldiers were shocked at the brutality of their Khan.

Temujin fled with his family, his generals (Jelme, Bo'orchu and Chiluan) and a small group of supporters and soldiers. History is unclear about where he went and how he survived. No documented evidence exists of what happened to him over the next 10 years, till 1197 A.D. For his followers, foes and well-wishers, at that point in time, the prophecy yet again seemed like a false prediction. The Great Khan-to-be was now the Khan who never was.

THE TRIBAL CONFEDERATION OF THE CENTRAL ASIAN STEPPE BEFORE TEMUJIN BORJIGIN

At the end of the 12th Century and beginning of the 13th Century A.D., central Asia was home to a number of wandering tribes. Starting a few hundred miles north of Beijing in the Chinese mainland, modern day Mongolia was home to 37 tribes, divided majorly into two categories: biological descendants of Bodonchar Munkhag (a 1st Century Mongolian warlord and founder of the "House of Borjigin") and his non-biological descendants. Till they were united in 1206 A.D., these tribes were known for flaky alliances, backstabbing and repeated infighting. Members of different tribes would intermingle at the risk of in-fighting because of petty differences.

While the title Khan or Qan is bestowed only on a leader elected by a confederation of tribes, before their unification, each tribe would have its own Khan. Each Khan would have his own agenda and seldom would they agree to stand by each other. When they did agree to do so, most often it would be with the intention of stabbing the other in the back the moment their tribe's interests would be served. Over time, some tribes had become more powerful than others. The powerful ones would form alliances with the lesser tribes, thus, creating a confederation. During the later half of the 12th century, there were 5 major tribal confederations, namely the Keraites, the Khamag Mongols, the Naimans, the Merkits and the Tatars. The Keraites and Khamag Mongols were on peaceful terms with each other. The Naimans, the Merkits and the Tatars were not aligned together, but they shared a common rivalry with the Keraites and the Khamag Mongols.

Certain parts of the Central Asian Steppe (which was the Mongolian mainland) was under the control of the Jin dynasty, which was established in China. They repeatedly made sure that the infighting among the different tribal confederations continued as they could attack and loot different parts of the country whenever they wanted. The Central Asian Steppe was a difficult territory to rule because of the cold weather and lack of vegetation and animals. To control the tribes here required long excursions and even longer battles. The Jin dynasty (Western Xia) wanted to establish control here but without expending too many of its resources. When the Tatars handed over Ambaghai Khan, leader of the Khagan Mongols, to the Jins for execution, it sowed the seeds of a long standing rivalry between the Tatars and the Khagan Mongols. The Khagan Mongols and Keraites would form frequent alliances to fight against Naimans, Merkits and Tatars.

The tribes had never been united even though together they could stand as a formidable force against the foreign Jin dynasty that had repeatedly subjugated the tribes to unfair trade practices, mass killings and looting.

THE EARLY YEARS OF TEMUJIN BORJIGIN AND HIS RISE TO POWER

Temujin Borjigin, born to the House of Borjigin royalty, was the eldest son of the Khan of the Khamag Mongol confederation. His birth had a touch of destiny attached to it. When he exited his mother's womb, he was clutching a blood clot in his hand. In Mongol myth, it is believed that he who is born with a blood clot in his hand is destined to be a great ruler. Maybe the greatest of all.

His father, Chief Yesugei saw this as a sign and, from a young age, taught Temujin the ways of the warrior. He was taught many lessons including horse riding, sword play, archery, clemency and diplomacy, among others. During these early years, Temujin became good friends with the son of another Khan. His name was Jamukha. Jamukha belonged to another tribe (the *Jadaran)* within the Khamag Mongol

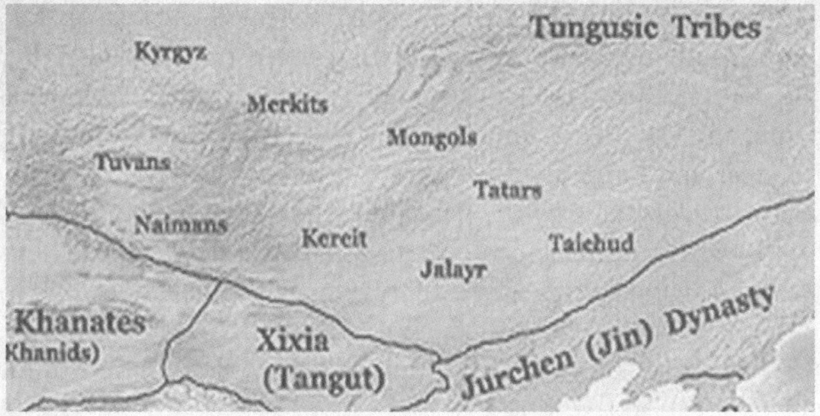

Mongolian Tribal Confederations till 1207 A.D.

confederation. Despite the difference in social status, they trained together as children. They grew very close and swore allegiance to one another as each other's *anda* (sworn blood brother). They swore that when each of them was Khan of their own tribes, they would rule as one, a force greater than any other that mankind had known. As children, they were certain that their destinies were intertwined. They were inseparable till Chief Yesugei decided to get Temujin married to a girl named Borte. As part of the marriage, Temujin had to serve in Borte's father's household till he was capable enough to have his own *yurt* (hut) for his wife and himself. The sworn blood brothers were separated. Temujin was 9 years old.

For the next 10 years, all that Temujin had learnt would be put to the test. Shortly after his marriage, his father was poisoned by a band of travelling Tatars, sworn enemies of the Khamag Mongols. Following this, his family were discarded by the Khamag Mongol confederation. They were ejected from the tribal confederation and were forced live in the wild, away from everything they had known to be familiar. Temujin returned to care for his family who were now living like nomads, surviving off of wild fruit and carcasses of dead animals. Jamukha urged his father to take them in, but the tribe were against it and in the entire confederation, they were treated as outcasts.

Temujin's mother, Lady Hoelun, revealed the reason for the tribe's animosity against their family to him when he was older. Lady Hoelun originally belonged to the Merkits tribe, another sworn enemy of the Khamag Mongols. In fact, Yesugei had kidnapped her and forcefully married her. This was not acceptable by the tribe, but since Yesugei belonged to the royal Borjigin blood line, no one could defy him. When he died, it was a measure of revenge for the whole tribal confederation to discard the "mixed bloods" from the tribe. This was a lesson in understanding the people that he would have to lead in the future.

Till he came of age, Temujin slowly learned many other lessons. One of them was learning to escape from tight situations. When he had been captured by the Taichiuds (one of the main tribes in the Khamag Mongol confederation), he escaped with the help of one of their own. He learned a great lesson in how empathy can drive a man's actions. Not only did he escape, he was given a horse and a bag full of lamb meat for his journey. Another lesson he learnt was how to reward loyalty. When his horses (the most prized possession of any Mongol) were stolen, he pursued them alone. During

A Traditional Mongolian Yurt

his pursuit, he was helped by a shepherd named Bo'orchu. When they got the horses back, he offered one as a reward to Bo'orchu. But Bo'orchu refused and exclaimed that his loyalty was not for sale. From then on, Bo'orchu remained by Temujin's side. Soon, he had more trustworthy people surrounding him, who were awed by his desire, conviction and "the fire in his eyes".

In 1180 A.D., Temujin established good relations with a ruling Khan. Toghrul, the *Khan* of the Keraite tribal confederation, was *anda* (sworn blood brother) to Yesugei, Temujin's father. In those days, an *anda* was a sworn bond till death and beyond. When Temujin approached Toghrul, he was welcomed with open arms and Toghrul hailed his survival instincts. He exclaimed how good a protector he had been of his family. In return, Temujin presented the great Khan with a sable jacket that he had received as a dowry in his marriage to Borte and offered to become a vassal tribe to the Keraites. His gift and offer were happily accepted.

In 1181 A.D., Borte was kidnapped from his *yurt* by Merkits, as revenge for when Yesugei had kidnapped Lady Hoelun. This action resulted in igniting the legendary rage that had, so far, resided deep inside the future Genghis Khan. Temujin didn't just want to rescue Borte, he wanted to destroy the Merkit tribal confederation altogether. He had decided that there could be no peace with them. Temujin went to Toghrul and asked for his help to eradicate their mutual enemy. Toghrul gave Temujin 20,000 troops and his blessing. But before he could leave, Temujin was instructed to ride North with his generals and find the Jadaran tribe.

Toghrul told him that his friend awaited him there. Temujin knew who it was. He rode North with untameable fervour and completed a 5 day ride in 3 days. When he reached, Jamukha, his sworn blood brother, his *anda,* received him with open arms. They feasted together and Temujin laid out his plan. Jamukha assembled 10,000 more troops and joined Temujin as they rode back to Toghrul to collect the 20,000 Keraite troops who waited for their commander.

When they reached the Merkit confederation camp, it was not a battle. It was an extermination. Over a few days, the Mongols, Keraites and Jadarans laid the Merkits to waste. Very few survivors remained. Those who did survive were turned into slaves. Temujin rescued Borte and rode back to his home. On the way back, Temujin was inseparable from Jamukha. They slept under the same tree, with the same blanket. They spoke like young children and argued on trivial matters, only to annoy the other. They again vowed to remain eternally faithful, as they separated and headed to their individual camps.

The victory over the Merkits had spread the legend of Temujin across all tribes. In essence, Temujin had arrived and could command armies now. In Mongol culture, shamanism was given great respect and the words of Shamans were believed as they were seen as messengers from the "Eternal Blue Sky". The followers would pray to the sky, considering it as "Eternal Heaven". In 1186 A.D., at a confluence attended by Toghrul, Jamukha and Temujin, a shaman named Kokochu, in his seemingly possessed state, professed that the "Eternal Blue Sky" had elected its leader and it would be Temujin Borjigin. With Toghrul's support, Temujin was elected the Khan of all the Mongols. He was rechristened with the name Genghis Khan. He was hailed as the Khan who was favoured by the Gods and men alike. His diplomacy and strategic brilliance had not been presented to the world yet. In his inner circle, his words were followed like royal decree. He would listen to his family and acted to protect them. This belief of his slowly began to permeate in the way he commanded and organised his soldiers, generals and followers.

Jamukha saw this as a betrayal by his sworn blood brother. They had agreed to rule together but now his brother seemed happy being elected the sole king of all the Mongols. When Genghis asked Jamukha to join him, Jamukha refused as he wanted to be named Khan as well. "As there can be only one sun in the sky, there can only be one Khan for our people". Jamukha turned his back to his sworn blood brother. He prepared to stake his claim to the throne. A backlash was in the offing. In 1187 A.D., with 30,000 troops, Jamukha brought the fight to Genghis doorstep. This battle was called The Battle of Dalan Balzhut.

The typical design of a Shaman's drum

Within a few days, Jamukha had decisively defeated the new Khan of the Mongols. Genghis was forced to flee with his family, his generals and few hundred troops. Jamukha had quelled the rise of the new Khan. Now, Jamukha could now stake his claim to the throne. Immediately after the victory, he ordered his troops to find the remaining followers and soldiers of Genghis. When they were brought to him, he ordered they be burnt alive in 70 cauldrons. This sent shockwaves across both camps. His first action after defeating Genghis was so disturbing that many of his own followers to flee from his camp and join Genghis.

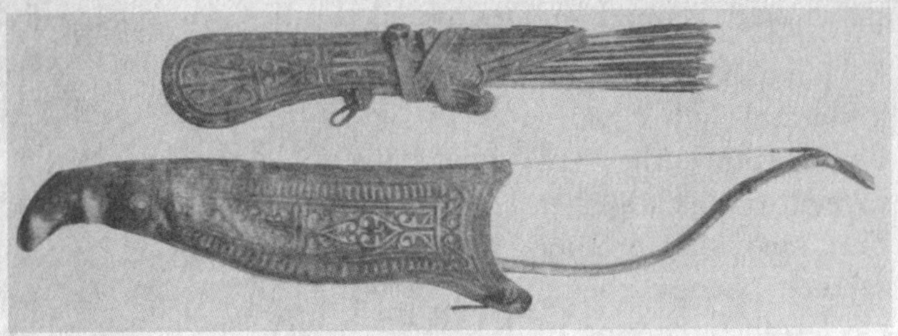

Typical Mongolian Bow and Arrow as displayed in the British Museum of Medieval Antiquities and Ethnography

After 10 years rebuilding his ranks and strength, in 1197 A.D., Genghis resurfaced and, in alliance with Toghrul and the remaining Khamag Mongols, decimated the Tatars. The Jin dynasty saw this as a great victory and rewarded both Toghrul and Genghis as vassal rulers. To Genghis', this was a way to understand the actual enemy of the Mongols. He understood their definition of vassal Kingdoms and how the Jins expected them to function. The Jin dynasty would eventually fall after repeated attacks by Genghis Khan's Golden Horde a few years later.

With the Tatars defeated, over the next 4 years, he reined terror on the Naimans, the remaining Merkits and the Tanguts. During these battles, after the enemy had been defeated, Genghis did not order the slaughter of the remaining soldiers. He gave them the opportunity to join his ranks. He did not want any animosity among the true and natural born Mongols. He wanted all Mongols to work in unison to form a formidable army. This was unprecedented and it took many by surprise. Many were happy to join the ranks of Genghis Khan's army. He adopted children of war and put them under the care of his mother, Lady Hoelun, and his wife, Lady Borte, thus garnering the reputation of being benevolent towards children.

Genghis shared the spoils of war with his troops and generals. He never kept any valuable possession for himself which did not have a strategic purpose. His followers were more than happy to follow him because he practiced meritocracy. To be promoted to the rank of a General, it was no longer necessary to descend from the lineage of a warrior. Even herdsmen, farmers, shepherds and hunters who proved their mettle in the field of battle would be promoted to the higher rank. The image of Genghis Khan, among the Mongols was that of a "ruthless warrior and a rational leader".

In 1201 A.D., as Genghis grew more and more powerful, Toghrul could feel his influence diminishing. His son, Senggum (influenced by Jamukha), poisoned his mind against Genghis and wanted to his father to have Genghis assassinated. Even though Genghis had always remained loyal to Toghrul, the Khan of the Keraites could not say no to his only son. Soon, he became uncooperative with Genghis. When Toghrul refused to give his daughter in marriage to Jochi, Genghis' eldest son, it was seen as a grave insult. Now, war was imminent. Toghrul sought Jamukha's help in his fight against Genghis. The same year, 13 tribes (not aligned with Genghis) assembled a *kurultai* (a political and military council) and elected Jamukha as their leader. Jamukha was now ready to take the fight to Genghis once again.

The Mongol Coin

This time, Genghis was more than prepared. His army was now 60,000 strong, most of them horse mounted archers who were equally good with their swords. But bloodshed was not something Genghis wanted until it was absolutely necessary. Genghis sent an emissary to Toghrul with a message that he still looked up to Toghrul, the great Khan of the Keraites and equivalent to his own father. If there was any way to avoid war, he was willing to listen. Toghrul wanted to discuss this with Jamukha but the newly crowned Khan was ready to go to war against Genghis. While Jamukha relied on those who belonged to a lineage of warriors to serve his army, Genghis had accepted even herdsmen and shepherds to join the ranks of his army if they would work hard and learn the ways of Mongol combat. Not only were Genghis' troops greater in number, but they had greater motivation and believed in the will of their leader.

War began early in 1202 A.D. After a series of battles, over 3 years, Genghis, as the killing blow, sent 8000 horse mounted warriors to finish off the Keraites. Many Keraites abandoned their posts and either fled or offered their services to the Mongol army. Toghrul was forced to flee North where he was killed by a soldier who failed to recognize him. When Genghis discovered Toghrul's body, he ordered that he be buried with the highest honour in the ancestral ground of the Mongols.

Since the war had begun, many generals and soldiers abandoned Jamukha. They went over to Genghis to join his ranks. Genghis could now tell the difference between those who were loyal and those who would betray (even their own Khan) to survive. Those who came to Genghis to serve him but would not betray their former Khan were wilfully accepted in the army. One such man was Subutai, who led Genghis' Horde to many successful campaigns across Europe and Asia. On the other hand, those who came to serve Genghis and divulged important secrets of Jamukha to Genghis were summarily executed.

In 1206 A.D., Jamukha had been defeated comprehensively. He was betrayed by his own men and handed over to Genghis' troops. Genghis understood that Jamukha's morale had

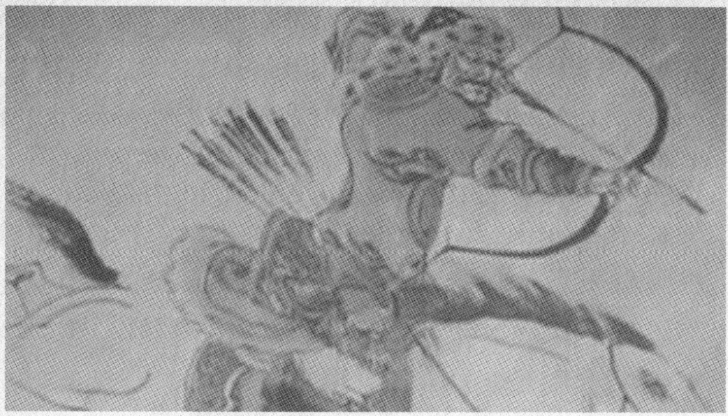

A Mongolian warrior on horseback

never been lower and this would be the best opportunity to secure his loyalty. Genghis had those who betrayed Jamukha immediately beheaded. In a council, Genghis sat with Jamukha and offered him support and friendship. He was willing to let the events of the past go and embrace Jamukha as his brother once again. Genghis told Jamukha that he still envisioned the both of them ruling the world together.

Even though it was an enticing offer, Jamukha's pride would not allow him to accept. He said to him again like he had said many years ago before their first battle, "As there can be only one sun in the sky, there can only be one Khan for our people". He asked for a noble bloodless death, which meant his back would be broken and not a single drop of blood would be spilt. Jamukha was buried in the ancestral ground of the Mongols by Genghis with the golden belt Jamukha had given him to seal their brotherhood, when they were children.

After Jamukha's demise, Genghis stood as the sole ruler of all Mongols. A formidable combination of strategic brilliance, horrifying terror and a horde of hundreds of thousands made the perfect combination for the coming of the largest empire ever to walk the earth. The time for petty battles was over. Now, the united Mongols looked beyond their own borders to foreign lands to capture land, destroy empires, eradicate dynasties and establish their monopoly on all known land-based trade routes.

At 44 years of age, in 1206 A.D., with no one to oppose him and no one with the influence and respect that he commanded, Genghis Khan was elevated to the status of the first ever Mongol *Khagan*, the King of Kings. His reign had officially begun.

THE MONGOLIAN EMPIRE UNDER THE RULE OF GENGHIS KHAN

MISSION: To unite all Mongolian tribes into a united confederation that would continue conquering to form the largest contiguous empire in the world and beyond.

MILITARY TECHNIQUES AND FORMATIONS

Genghis Khan wanted an army like no other. Warriors who could fight till the last member of their body had strength. Since horses were the most prized possession of any Mongol, he envisioned an army that would ride horseback with the same proficiency as they would fight on the ground. He made Jelme and Bo'orchu, his close aides, in charge of mastering these techniques and disseminating them to the army. Through their training, almost all of the army became proficient in riding horseback, standing on horseback and shooting arrows while seated/standing on a galloping horse. The very sight of such a warrior was so terrifying that it sent many soldiers fleeing even before an arrow had been drawn. During times of siege and war, each soldier was expected to maintain 3-4 horses. This was to make sure that none of the horses are too tired from the long travels and battles.

Mongol forces, made up of skilled warriors well trained in marksmanship and horsemanship, were characterized by absolute discipline, a well-understood chain of command, an excellent communications system, superior mobility, and an effective tactical organization. Never very large, it relied on superior tactics and speed, and was like a well-disciplined cavalry which moved rapidly, adapted quickly to changing situations and followed complex battle strategies. The core of Genghis Khan's army consisted of only 23,000 horsemen who fought with composite bows and hand axes and protected themselves with waterproof leather armour. The Mongol army was divided into units (each with its own commander) of 10-man squads (arvan), 100-man companies (zuun), 1,000-man battalions (Mingghan) and 10,000 men divisions (tumens), with an imperial guard of 10,000 soldiers protecting the Khan and important generals. The imperial guards were trained in the institution called Kheshig, which was meant for the most elite of all warriors. Some of the greatest war generals of the Mongol Empire graduated from the Kheshig before joining the army or the imperial guard.

RELIGIOUS TOLERANCE AND THE YASSA

News of Genghis Khan's practices soon spread across the Central Asian Steppe, across all the 37 tribes that inhabited the plains. As many flocked to join his ranks, he observed another conflict arising among his followers. Each tribe had their own religious practices. As many as 20 religions existed in his ranks. There were those who would take insults very seriously and the in-fighting would begin again. In the past, these religious inclinations had been dealt with by the Khan by imposing one religion on all followers thus giving rise to dissent among the people of different religious

THE POLITICAL CLIMATE OF THE MONGOLIAN EMPIRE

Political State: A large tribal confederation initially consisting of 20 of the 37 tribes of Mongolian descent.

Geographical Extent: The Mongol empire stretched from the Sea of Japan in the east till the Caspian Sea in the West, forming the largest contiguous empire in history.

"Yassa" was the law: Genghis Khan created a list of laws which had to be followed within the Mongol empire. These laws governed matters of matrimony, inheritance, treatment of animals, looting, honourable titles, among other things.

Autocratic Leadership: The Mongol Empire had only one unanimous leader, Genghis Khan, who would consult his generals and advisors. There were no ministers or other decision makers.

inclinations. Genghis took a different approach. He made every religion acceptable in his camp. He banned fighting because of religious differences and those found indulging in it would be severely reprimanded. Soon, the infighting reduced and tolerance was practiced by almost everyone in the Mongol camp.

To give the right of free existence to any and all religions, they had to be reinforced with certain laws and regulations. In the absence of such laws, there would be anarchy. Genghis Khan thus created a written code of law called Yassa. Yassa was initially a secret code of conduct enforced at times of war, but later they were included in cultural and lifestyle conventions. Genghis' second son, Chagatai was made in charge of enforcing and execution of the laws. Pertaining to religion, the edicts were "all religions are to be respected and that no preference is to be shown to any of them. All this he commanded in order that it might be agreeable to Heaven". Apart from this, there were laws governing everyday life, enlisting in the army (all males were mandatorily required to do so), treatment of slaves, hunting of animals, election of leaders, plundering and looting rules, among many other topics.

THE YAM: THE WORLD'S FIRST ORGANISED MAIL SYSTEM

A serious problem faced by all rulers at that time was the validity of information that was given to them. Because of the high likelihood of betrayal, no intelligence could be trusted for too long. If enough time had passed, a message sent through a messenger, riding from one camp to the next, could become redundant by the time the message reached its intended recipient. Once the tribes had been reunited, this was one problem that Genghis Khan wanted to fix.

Even before taking the throne, Genghis Khan ordered the setting up of outposts that were meant to store supplies and have messengers to relay intelligence to different locations across the Central Asian Steppe. With this system, the Mongol Empire's pace of transmitting information became faster than any other information transmission system known to exist. Intelligence could now be treated as valid and decisive choices were no longer left to chance. Once an invasion or rebellion was spotted, Genghis would have been made aware of it within days, instead of weeks, because of the message relaying system. When Genghis Khan was hailed as the "universal ruler", he immediately ordered increasing the number of outposts across the Mongol Empire and keeping them stocked with enough messengers and supplies.

This system would become a great strength for the Mongols once they had established their control over the Silk Road to spread messages across the empire about rogue traders, illegal activities and impending attacks. This system was called the Yam route. Apart from just transmitting messages, because of the stocking of supplies and resources, the Mongol warriors could complete journeys much faster, without spending time on pitching camps and hunting for food. The army could now move from outpost to outpost within days, never at the risk of starvation or surprise attacks.

THE ECONOMIC PROFILE OF THE MONGOLIAN EMPIRE

Primary Work: Animal husbandry and crop farming

Taxation: There were no taxes levied on members of the Mongol Empire. Traders on the Silk Road were taxed for the goods they were trading. The tax could be collected in currency or kind.

Looting was legal but controlled: Under Yassa, until the commander of a battalion gave clearance, no conquered territory could be looted by the warriors. Goods and currency acquired could be confiscated for the central reserve of the Mongol Empire.

Pax Mongolica: Roughly translated, it means the Mongolian Peace. Pax Monglica was a means to establish peaceful terms with neighbouring or conquered territories, predicated on favourable trade relations for the Mongols.

Currency: Numerous, but the most common currency was the Mongol Coin.

Death Sentence for Forgery: Currency forgery was considered a grave crime and would be punishable by death.

1206 A.D.- 1218 A.D.: VASSAL KINGDOMS, THE LEGEND OF SUBUTAI AND THE PRECISION OF JEBE

In 1206 A.D., after the defeat of Jamukha, Genghis Khan was finally unanimously accepted as the leader of the united Mongol Khanate. By now, as many as 20 (of 37) tribes had come under the leadership of Genghis Khan. After his ascension, Genghis Khan's first target was the Western Xia (ruled by the Jin Dynasty) in mainland China. Under the pretext of hunting Nilga Senggum, son of Toghrul (Khan of the Keraite tribe), the Mongols began to conduct small scale raids on the area. The real reason for the raids was to slowly establish control over the Silk road that lay in the region of the Western Xia empire. First, the city of Ganzhou, then the garrison of Wuhai along the yellow river.

Subutai

Genghis withdrew in 1208 and planned a full scale invasion in 1209. In the first major invasion, Genghis razed as many as 20 cities to the ground before reaching the Xia capital of Yinchuan. But the walled, fortified capital was impossible to breach. In January 1210, after flooding the city, the city was nearly breached. Even though their efforts did not bear fruit, the Mongol invasion had done enough damage for the Western Xia's Jin Emperor Li Anquan to submit to Genghis Khan's will and pledged his loyalty the Mongol King. He agreed to pay a tribute to him and allow the Mongols to take control of the caravan routes along the Silk Road, thus, securing even more revenue.

Even though the Western Xia hadn't been completely defeated by the Mongols, Genghis had been advised to keep them as a vassal Kingdom in order to use them as a pathway to attack the Jin Dynasty to the south. This advice came from one of his most celebrated generals. His name was Subutai. He had risen through the ranks, from commoner to general, and had proven himself to be an able general. He was described by Genghis Khan as a "dog of war" and respectfully referred to as "Subutai the valiant", his most capable tactician. Subutai was as cunning as he was loyal. During the return from the invasion of the Western Xia, he conversed with Genghis' about how the politics of a region having a direct impact on its attacking strategy. His observation: When the Jin ruler, Emperor Xuanzong, refused to help the Western Xia during the Mongols invasion, the Emperor's actions were a clear sign of their militaristic ineptitude. Hence, on Subutai's recommendation, immediately after Western Xia had been established as a vassal, the Mongols attacked the Jin dynasty in the south. Over the next 3 years, the Mongols massacred hundreds of thousands of Jin troops and completely dismantled the dynasty. In 1215 A.D., Genghis Khan officially captured the capital city of Zhongdu. Emperor Xuanzong fled southwards, shifting the capital to the southern city of Kaifeng. The Jin dynasty's influence on central Asia had now been completely nullified.

THE MONGOLIAN EMPIRE'S SOCIAL NORMS

Religious Tolerance: there was acceptance of any and all religions among the Mongol people, a move that enhanced his popularity amongst his people

The Golden Horde: All men in the Mongol Empire were necessarily required to serve in the army. Many of them, regardless of background, rose up the ranks and became formidable warriors (like Subutai)

Visual art was appreciated: Visual arts were promoted among the Mongols. Also, artists from the conquered territories were sent back to the capital and their skills were harnessed.

Male-dominated polygamous society: Women were considered lower in status than men. Men were allowed to have multiple wives and concubines. Children from all wives would come under the care of the father.

Homosexuality was illegal: Homosexuality was considered illegal and was punishable by death.

Horses were the greatest assets and horse-riding ability was a necessity: In Mongol culture, the horse was considered the greatest asset for any tribesperson and the skill of horse riding was imperative, regardless of gender and age.

Subutai was hailed within the Mongol empire as the right hand of the great Khan and soon, he would cement his reputation as one of the greatest war generals to have ever lived by serving 2 more Khans after Genghis. In total, Subutai led and coordinated more than 70 successful Mongol invasions, including the legendary coordinated invasion of Poland and Hungary, 2 days apart, even though the 2 armies were 500 miles away from each other. It is difficult to imagine the Mongol war machine being as effective as it was without Subutai commanding them.

After 10 years of fighting and conquering the Western Xia and the Jin, the army had begun to tire and longed to go home. Genghis Khan and Subutai both felt that they should return home and chart out a course for the next conquest. The East and South had been largely secured and many more tribes were joining the Mongol ranks. Their leader was needed back home. On their journey, they discussed how they could exercise further control over the Silk Road, ensuring more revenue and goods. It was during the journey back that Genghis was made aware of an old enemy who had escaped and established his rule in the south western region called Qara Khitai. His name was Kuchlug and he was a Naiman prince who had escaped when the Naimans were purged by the Mongols. It seemed like an opportunity to usurp another Kingdom and a relatively easy conquest of another territory.

THE MONGILIAN EMPIRE'S TECHNOLOGICAL ADVANCES

Yam-The world's first mail system: Under Genghis Khan, the Mongol established the Yam route system of sending messages. This system made sure critical messages and intelligence reached Genghis and his generals faster than ever before.

Materials: Mongols lived off the earth and would use animal hides and natural materials. There is not much evidence of the casting or usage of metals other than for tips of spears and small blades. The Silk Road definitely brought certain definitely brought international technological advances to the Mongols.

Weapons: During the early years of Genghis Khan's rule, hand-made weapons were the norm including the Mongol bow. But after the conquest of Western Xia and the Jins, modern weapons like catapults and trebuchets were imported into the arsenal of the Mongols.

The Mongols were exhausted and Genghis feared that they may not be up for another conquest. But laying siege to the Qara Khitai would not be as exhausting as fighting the Xia or the Jins. Also, conquering Qara Khitai would give them a strategically advantageous position on the Silk Road as well as to stay close to the expanding and the disrespectful Khwarezimian Empire. It was imperative that they take the region and establish themselves there.

Genghis Khan's strategies were renowned and for this conquest, he chose a new one: change the established sentiment and overthrow the ruler. With 2 tumens (20,000 soldiers), he instructed another one of his generals, Jebe, to conquer the region and depose Kuchlug. Jebe, also known as "The Arrow", was told that 20,000 troops would not nearly be enough to cause an overthrow. He must cause internal dissension against their ruler. In the past, warriors from the region had pledged allegiance to Genghis Khan and more could follow. They waited for the chance to attack once the Kingdom was vulnerable. Jebe sent spies and agents into the

A 19th Century illustration of Jebe in the Battle of the Kalka River

towns and cities. Over 2 years, starting from 1216 A.D., they incited the people against their foreign ruler who had killed their true ruler and forcefully taken the throne. Slowly the sentiment towards their leader, Kuchlug, began to turn and most of the population swore allegiance to the great Genghis Khan. The opportunity to attack finally presented itself in 1218 A.D. and Jebe capitalized fully. With very few losses, the Mongols took over the large Qara Khitai region in a matter of weeks. Kuchlug had fled the moment he sensed the attack. But he couldn't get far. The whole populace had turned on Kuchlug and a group of hunters captured him in the Pamir Mountains as he was fleeing. They promptly handed him over to the Mongol soldiers who brought him to their general Jebe. Without saying a word or negotiating, Jebe beheaded him and took the head as a memento. In the summer of 1218 A.D., within 2 years, the complete conquest of Qara Khitai (a nation almost the size of modern day Mexico) was complete. The Mongols returned home, glorious and victorious.

1219 A.D.-1227 A.D.: THE KHWAREZMIAN EMPIRE BLITZKRIEG AND ATTAINING LEGENDARY STATUS

In the spring of 1219 A.D., an unprecedented event occurred. Across the rain starved plains and arid deserts of the Central Asian steppe, spring had come. Grass emerged from the ground. Trees were filled with leaves, fruits and flowers. The region was blessed with plentiful rainfall. The animals grazed freely and galloped happily. Many said this was the first rainfall in 100 years. When the Mongol army returned from their conquest in the East, they were welcomed as saviours who had brought relief to the plains and the Eternal Blue Sky had blessed their conquest. Genghis Khan, now, was not just revered as a great ruler, but also seen as a blessing from heaven for the Mongol people. There were many gifts bestowed on Genghis from his followers. Genghis respectfully accepted but asked the people to not send any further gifts. He worked for their prosperity and whatever they gained was theirs to keep. For the next 8 years, the region received regular rainfall. The arid lands became vibrant and the animals grew significantly in number. It was all attributed to their great Khan and his prophetic rise to power.

Genghis turned his attention towards establishing strong trade relations with neighbouring empires. In order to have strong control over the Silk Road, Genghis had to reach out to the Khwarezmian empire. Located to the south-west of the Mongolian stronghold, the Qara Khitan region shared a border with the North Eastern reach of the Khwarezmian Empire. Genghis desired a peaceful trade relationship with the Muslim empire. Once the celebrations of the spring were over, Genghis sent a caravan of emissaries for Sultan Ala ad-Din Muhammad, the ruler of the Khwarezmian Empire. It was a peaceful envoy meant to bring a message to the Sultan: "I am master of the lands of the rising sun while you rule those of the setting sun. Let us conclude a firm treaty of friendship and peace." But the message never reached the Sultan. The convoy was arrested in Khwarezmian city of Otrar. The governor of the city suspected them to be spies of Genghis Khan and kept them under arrest till there were further instructions from his Sultan.

The Mongolian Empire in 1206 AD

News of this reached Genghis Khan and he acted immediately. He sent another ambassador but this time, he sent an ambassador who was Muslim with two other high ranking Mongols. He wanted to firmly send the message that he did not want to fight and that the Mongol empire is a thoroughly tolerant regime. He also wanted the people of the caravan in Otrar be set free immediately and governor be punished suitably for his impudence by the Sultan. Thinking of the Sultan to be a rational man with rational advisors, Genghis began preparations to meet the Sultan himself if it was required.

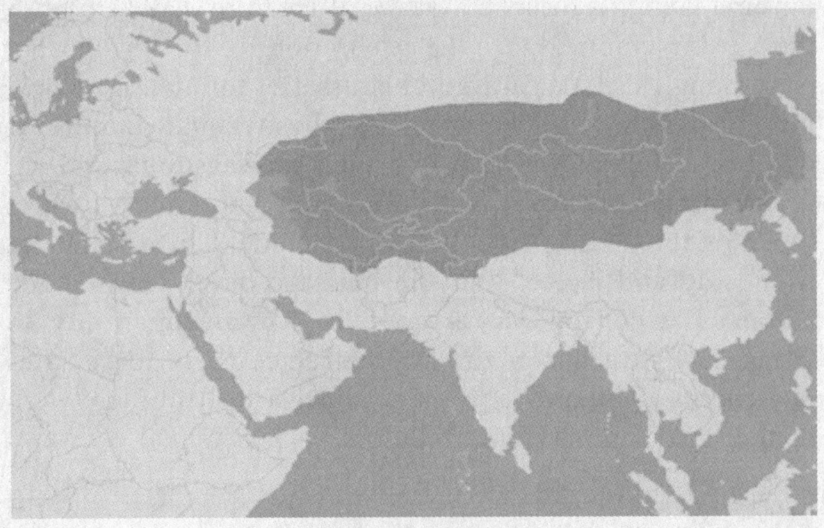

The Mongolian Empire in 1227 AD

Soon, the ambassadors returned but only 2 out of the 3 who had been sent. The heads of the high ranking Mongols had been forcefully shaven and the Muslim ambassador had been beheaded by order of the Sultan. The members of the caravan had been murdered too. This was an act that deeply enraged Genghis Khan as envoys or ambassadors were considered "sacred and inviolable" messengers. As the word of this spread across the camp, the troops were ready to rally behind Genghis to annihilate the Muslim empire to the west.

Within days, intelligence was collected and preparations were made for the invasion and planned annihilation of the Khwarezmian Empire.

The invasion lasted 2 years. In 1219 A.D., the Mongols crossed the Tian Shan Mountains. The Sultan was anticipating a united attack from the north. But the Mongols broke into strategic units that would raid individual cities. It was an organized plan to divide and conquer. Once the cities had been taken, the survivors would be separated into "those were taller than the height of a horse cart and those who were shorter". Those who were taller were massacred or used as human shields in future battles. The rest were converted into followers and slaves of the Mongols. The army of the Khwarezmian Empire was 400,000 strong but paled in comparison to the 800,000 army of the Mongols, led by Subutai and Jebe. Within a year, the Khwarezmian army had become disorganized and fragmented trying to quell invasions in the different cities of the empire. They fell like flies while facing the Mongolian Horde.

By the end of 1220 A.D., only 20,000 troops remained who were in charge of guarding the fortified capital city of Samarkhand. After Genghis took the nearby city of Bukhara, he focussed his attention towards Samarkhand. The Mongol troops assembled together and finally laid siege to the capital and after 3 months of constant fighting, broke the defences of the city and took over. The Sultan had fled to an island in the Caspian Sea. Jochi (Genghis Khan's son) and his war party pursed him but when they found him he had died in isolation on an island in the Caspian Sea. By early 1221 A.D., the Khwarezmian Empire was completely destroyed and the land mass from Qara Khitai till the Caspian Sea had come under the control of Genghis Khan and the Mongols.

Jochi, Jebe and Subutai had executed Genghis Khan's plan perfectly. During the invasion, the Mongols are estimated to have massacred 1.5 million people, including civilians. With this victory, the Silk Road's entire eastern wing had now come under the control of Genghis Khan and the Mongols. The legend of the terrifying ability of Mongol Horde had now spread to the West, to the countries in Eastern Europe, including Georgia, Crimea, Kievan Rus and Volga Bulgaria. The Mongolian Horde was ambitious and Genghis would not stop them from conquering more. The war parties and their generals were given new orders, to drive out the princes and plunder the nations of Crimea, Georgia and Kievan Rus. In 5 years, each of these nations and their leaders would fall to the relentless and terrifying assault of the Mongolian Horde.

By 1227 A.D., at different times of the year, each of these European nations had come under Mongolian control. The civilians and remaining armies had knelt to Genghis Khan and pledged allegiance to him. It is believed in Crimea the army surrendered without any resistance at the sight of an army of horse mounted archers riding in their direction. Once all these territories were secured and turned into vassal Kingdoms, Genghis Khan returned to his home and, with his trusted war general Subutai, began planning for his second invasion of the Western Xia who had not paid their tribute and had begun rebellion against Mongol rule in the region.

STRENGTH-WEAKNESS-OPPORTUNITY-THREAT (SWOT) ANALYSIS OF TEMUJIN BORJIGIN

STRENGTHS	WEAKNESSES
1. **"Genghis Khan":** This was a cognomen given to Temujin Borjigin by his followers, which literally meant "Universal Ruler" 2. **Visionary:** Even though his initial years were marred with poverty and repeated defeats, he had a grander vision of a united Mongol empire, greater than anything mankind had seen so far 3. **Collectivist:** Temujin did not believe in divide and rule. Instead of massacring those he conquered, he made them join his ranks and serve under him 4. **Negotiator:** Temujin's formidable army and astute negotiation skills allowed him to maintain order along the largest land based trade route in the world called "The Silk Road" and make vassal Kingdoms all around Mongolia, till Europe.	1. **Savage Lust:** After he came to power, rape and sexual savagery became synonymous with Temujin and his troops. This reputation has contributed to the image of a barbarian king as he is remembered today 2. **God Complex:** Because of his rise to power at an early age and the prophecy associated with his birth, he always had a God complex that guided his actions and his eventual death, when he decided to enter the field of battle at a frail old age
OPPORTUNITIES	**THREATS**
1. **European and Pan-Asian Conquest:** During the 12th century, mainland Europe and Central Asia were still rather fragmented, ruled by individual Kingdoms or rulers. Even though Christianity was spreading in the west, Temujin's tolerant religious practices and collectivist approach presented the opportunity to conquer or form alliances with those in the West and East 2. **Iron fist control of the Silk road:** Because the heart of the Silk road lay in Mongol territory, it was one of the greatest opportunities for Temujin to establish his authority in both the East and the West 3. **Slow Rise of Central Asian Empire:** After the rule of Atilla the Hun who had temporarily united nomadic races for wide conquests, Temujin knew a united Kingdom could ensure a much longer reign for the Mongols 4. **Fulfil the prophecy:** From the day of his birth, Temujin had been thought of as potentially the greatest ruler ever to live. His greatest opportunity was to unite the nomadic tribes of Mongolia and Central Asia under this prophesy	1. **Jamukha:** The only one to rival his influence and ability as a warrior king was Jamukha, his sworn blood brother. Till 1206 A.D., Temujin would not rise to the level he desired because of Jamukha 2. **Romans in the West:** Throughout his reign, there was a threat of incursions from the west who considered him a savage king without God or any guiding morals. This threat continued long after his death as they tried to destroy any documentation of Temujin's reign to change his image in the eyes of modern Mongolia. 3. **Internal Dissent:** Some of Temujin's policies on how to deal with traitors were seen as brutal and unfair. The threat of dissent and potential rebellion was a constant (but low lying) threat

WHY IS TEMUJIN BORJIGIN A VISIONARY LEADER?

Visionary leadership is the act of leading one's followers with a clear vision for collective action. A visionary leader is aware of the long term goal as well as the path that needs to be taken to achieve it. Visionary leaders are settled with their actions, decisions and diction. They are generally experienced strategists who know how to lead under diverse and trying circumstances. Practical awareness, alluring confidence and a headstrong nature are the telling characteristics of a visionary leader.

In a world where violence conveyed more than words could and the world was still for the taking, a visionary leader was one who wanted to conquer the world with a systematic plan. Body count was a matter of pride, not outrage. In the Central Asian Steppe, the tribal confederations of Mongolia were either fighting the Jin Dynasty in the East or they were fighting among themselves. For more than a century, many Khans had risen and fallen. None had the power or influence to unite them all.

Temujin Borjigin had a stellar and an untameable spirit. This is clear from his exploits while escaping captivity, negotiating with rival Khans and ruthless ambition while acquiring foreign Kingdoms. From a young age, he dreamt of reaching the stature of his father as Khan of his own tribe. His natural ability as a leader took him much beyond that.

Temujin's vision evolved with time. Initially he wanted to gain power as a worthy warrior capable of leading his own tribe by earning recommendation from a worthy leader. Toghrul was that leader and Genghis' victory over the Merkits solidified his reputation. Once he had achieved that, his legend became widely known, thus, prompting the unprecedented nomination to be the King of Kings. In the 10 years that followed, Temujin sharpened his expectations as a Khan and optimized tactics for battle and negotiation.

He realized that the key to a sustained rule is to be feared and respected; the former more than the latter.

Temujin Borjigin conquered many people and lands. He inspired a great army of strong warriors whose legend is unmatched. His desire to be a ruler without vanity gave him like God-like status among his indigenous followers. He envisioned a united future for his country. In a change from practices of the past, he rewarded merit and denounced aristocratic privileges. He created a society of united Mongolian tribes, segregated by social status and military rankings. He had seen the long term problems of rewarding someone because of their parentage and how the rest of society perceives it as an unfair privilege.

Temujin created a society with religious pluralism and thus was tolerant of many religious practices. Growing up, he had seen how many Khans and tribes had fought and nearly decimated each other because one could not tolerate the other's religious beliefs. It was a wise move by Temujin and it worked well to bind the different tribes. At that time, one of the greatest personal motivators was the appeasement of the Gods and the freedom to indulge in individual religious practices.

During his reign, the Mongols wanted to replicate the greatness of the Huns of Central Asia. The days of barbarianism were still very much in vogue in the Central Asian Steppe region. They needed a leader who they could look up to as an unstoppable warrior with an indomitable spirit. They demanded a leader who was a world conqueror, in legend and ability. The touch of destiny associated with his birth (the blood clot incident) allowed his legend to travel much farther than he did. In 2 decades of ruling, Temujin Borjigin laid the foundation for the largest contiguous empire in human history. His vision would last beyond his days and his children and grandchildren (Ogodei and Kublai) realized his dream during their reign.

GENGHIS KHAN'S DEATH

In 1227 A.D., before undertaking the second invasion of the Western Xia region, Genghis Khan gathered his sons and notified them of how the empire would be divided among them. Jochi, his eldest son, would not inherit his father's title as Khan of all Mongols. Jochi's parentage was always a topic of debate as it was alleged that he was conceived when his mother, Lady Borte, was kidnapped by the Merkits. This accusation of being the bastard child, especially by his younger brother Chagatai, added to his already flaring temper. Thus, Genghis Khan decided to give the title of Khan to Ogodei, his third son who was known for diplomacy and possessing the calm required of a strong leader.

It can be argued since this announcement was made before Genghis Khan left, he may have been aware of his deteriorating health condition because of his age. But there is no substantial evidence in this regard. His death is still a matter of debate, with different versions told by different sources. Each source has its own prejudice or propaganda associated with it. One account says while fighting against the Western Xia, an arrow pierced Genghis Khan's right arm but it did not stop him in any way. He continued marauding. But on the 3rd day after sustaining the injury, a fever set in. This was followed by gangrene. Finally, when he passed away, his body was so badly mutilated that he was encased in a metal frame and taken back to his family.

Another account states that during the invasion, Genghis Khan decided to take a Western Xia princess as his slave. When he took her took his bed chamber, she swiftly pulled out a small blade, hidden on the inside of her thigh, and stabbed him in the neck. She muffled his screams with a pillow while he bled to death. When they found them, the princess had a smile on her face, claiming to have annihilated a God. She was executed and Genghis Khan was immediately taken home to his family for his burial.

There are other accounts stating that he had been killed in battle and another that he had fallen from his horse while hunting and broke his neck. It is one's best guess which one of these accounts is true.

GENGHIS KHAN'S LAST KNOWN LOCATION

Similar to the most influential leaders in past who belonged to Central Asia, like Gilgamesh and Atilla the Hun, Genghis Khan had made his followers aware that upon his death, he was to be buried in an unmarked grave in an undiscoverable location. This was the custom of his tribe and the Royal House of Borjigin. Consequently, like the cause of his death, his final resting place is also a topic for debate.

According to one source, when he died, his body was taken to the place of his birth. Once there, the Mongols built a dam to change the course of a part of the Onon River. Once the river had been diverted, his grave was dug and his unmarked coffin was placed in the grave. Once buried, the dam was broken and the river resumed its course, hiding his resting place forever.

Another account states that his grave was stampeded over by many horses, and that trees were then planted over the site, and the permafrost also did its part in hiding the burial site. According to the same story, the funeral escort killed anyone and anything in their path to conceal where he was finally buried.

GENGHIS KHAN'S RAPE AND KILL COUNT

Temujin Borjigin aka Genghis Khan has the unsavoury reputation of being history's most savage and lustful dictator. The cause for astonishment is not just the number of people he killed, but also the number of illegitimate children he fathered. He raped an ungodly number of women, begetting so many children that, today, according to different studies, 0.5% of the world's male population are direct descendants of Genghis Khan (carrying his Y chromosome). The number was estimated to be 16 million male descendants in 2010 i.e. 1 in every 200 men.

Genghis Khan's kill count is a number that still sends shivers down many-a spine. Even though he almost always spared the lives of women and children, his decision to massacre men would vary depending on the militaristic and strategic advantage their survival could present. Even after practicing restraint in certain battles, his individual kill count still surpasses the population of many modern day countries. The figure, although disputed, safely ranges from 15 to 25 million people from 1187 A.D. to 1227 A.D.

TRANSACTIONAL LEADERSHIP

VLAD TEPES: THE VOIVODE WHO MASTERED THE ART OF PROFITABLY SHIFTING ALLIANCES

"Even if a snake is not poisonous, it should pretend to be venomous"

- Chanakya

VLAD TEPES a.k.a. VLAD DRACULA a.k.a VLAD THE IMPALER
(1431 A.D.- 1476 A.D.)

VOIVODE OF WALLACHIA
(1448, 1456-1462, 1476)

Vlad Tepes was the son of Vlad Dracul, a 2-time voivode (prince) of the principality of Wallachia and a member of the Christian "Order of the Dragon". Wallachia was the doorway to Europe for the growing Ottoman Empire as well as the doorway to the East for the established Kingdoms of Romania, Hungary and Bulgaria. Vlad Tepes was a 3-time voivode (prince) of Wallachia. Wallachia was the most important principality of Romanian kingdom.

Vlad hated the Ottomans and especially their leader, Sultan Mehmed the 2nd. His hatred stemmed from his forced servitude to the Ottomans (as tribute by his father to the Ottoman King) for 4 of his teenage years. While in captivity, he was forced to learn their ways, which he found oppressive and severely anti-Christian. He did not take kindly to those methods neither to the arrogant and privileged soon-to-be King, Sultan Mehmed the 2nd, son of the King. Vlad swore to kill him when he would be freed. The chance of going to war against the Ottomans appealed to Vlad's most basic instincts.

Vlad was warned by the Christian rulers of Europe to avoid war with the Ottomans at all costs. War was not profitable for the Christians at that time. They were still reeling under the losses and fallout from the collapse of the Byzantine Empire, better known as the Eastern Roman Empire, at the hands of the Ottoman Turks. The Ottomans had laid siege to Constantinople with an army of 150,000 strong and had succeeded, where Atilla the Hun had failed 1000 years ago. The Christian stronghold on Eastern Europe was loosening but war was hardly the feasible solution to the problem. King Matthias Corvinus, the King of Hungary and one of the few who aligned himself with Vlad, instructed him to comply and pay the tax that was demanded by the Ottomans and keep the peace for as long as possible.

When Sultan Mehmed's envoy arrived in Wallachia to collect the first payment of tax and discuss terms for the subsequent payments, they were not prepared for the treatment that Vlad had in mind for them. Vlad wanted to send a message to the Sultan, one that would remind Sultan that Vlad's childhood hatred for him not subsided. Not one bit. While in the presence of Vlad, when the two Ottoman messengers would not remove their turbans, Vlad asked why. Even though he knew why, he wanted to hear it from them. One of the ambassadors told him they had religious reasons and they were forbidden from taking the turban off in front of others. Calmly, Vlad nodded, acknowledging his answer. Then, with equal calm, he instructed his guards to pin the ambassador's heads to the table and nail their turbans into their heads, thus, making sure the turbans stay on permanently. The ambassadors died, screaming in pain. Their bodies were sent back to the Sultan.

War was now imminent and all allies had withdrawn support. Vlad, along with his army of about 30,000, was left unsupported to defend Wallachia and the Kingdom of Romania. With the Ottoman attack on the brink, a Greek envoy from the Sultan arrived in Wallachia and met with Vlad. The Sultan had sent an order for Vlad to come to Constantinople. This was part of a trap to capture Vlad when he crossed the Danube, on his way to Constantinople. But Vlad caught wind of this and ordered the execution of the envoy. Subsequently, as 10,000 Ottoman troops advanced through the mountains to reach Wallachia, Vlad's troops cut them off in a mountain pass, pinned them against the mountain and massacred them without much of a fight.

While others would've thought this to be a mistake that could incite the vicious rage of the Asia's largest empire, Vlad saw it as the first opportunity to strike fear into the heart of his opposition. Those Ottoman Turkic troops who had survived the mountain onslaught were brought back to Transylvania, another one of Vlad's strongholds within Romanian boundaries. Once there, the troops were stripped and publicly impaled. A wooden spike was oiled and inserted into the rectum of every soldier and pushed through his body till it came out through his mouth. This spike was erected in a public space for everyone to see the soldiers die an agonisingly slow death. This sent shockwaves to all Romanians. Soon after, the message reached the Sultan who was horrified and began preparations for a full scale war with an army as big as the one that took Constantinople, against his forever nemesis.

But Vlad had other plans. He knew meeting them face to face in the field of battle would be valiant but an effort that surely destroy him and his army. He had to be smart. He had to be cunning. Something that, ironically, the Ottomans had trained him well to be. Thus began Vlad's most effective guerrilla war against his former captors and his most hated enemy, Sultan Mehmed the 2nd.

THE HOUSE OF BASARAB AND THE PRINCIPALITY OF WALLACHIA BEFORE THE RULE OF VLAD TEPES

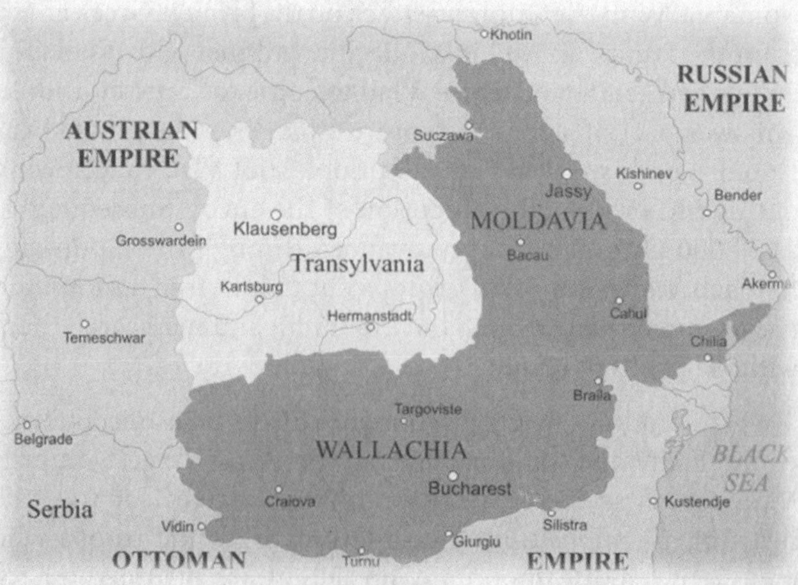

The Danubian Provinces

In the early 14th century, the Kingdom of Romania was under the suzerainty of the Kingdom of Hungary. King Charles the 1st, the Hungarian King at that time, had control over the principalities of Wallachia, Transylvania and Moldavia. These 3 areas were collectively called the "Danubian Principalities", as they were located along the lower Danube River. His rule and suzerainty in Wallachia was overthrown by Basarab the 1st in 1330 during the "Battle of Posada", where Basarab's army of peasants and foot archers defeated King Charles' army of 30,000 strong in the Wallachian mountainous region of Oltenia and Severin. In doing so, Basarab the 1st claimed the right to be called the first *voivode* (prince) of the independent principality of Wallachia.

With this victory, the name Basarab echoed through the Austrian, Hungarian and Ottoman Empire. The House of Basarab became the ruling family of the principality of Wallachia and led the way in the secession of Wallachia from the Kingdom of Hungary. Basarab the 1st was a staunch Christian and he envisioned the same for his successors. He aligned with the Byzantine Empire (or the Eastern European Empire) to christen Wallachia as a Christian Orthodox Kingdom. Further, Nicolae Alexandru, son of Basarab the 1st, chose the Byzantine model of government and converted the principality of Wallachia into an absolute monarchy. The princes' had absolute power, which was announced to be divinely ordained. The monarchy was also dynastic: the *voivodes* (princes) were to be elected by *boyars (the local land owning aristocracy)* from among the members of the ruling family, the Basarabs. It is believed that the elections were rigged by the different candidates of the Basarab House and the elections were a sham. The *voivode* who was favoured by the Pope in Constantinople would be elected, regardless of the results of the election.

The rule of the Basarabs continued long after the passing of Basarab the 1st. But in the early part of the 14th century,

Dan the 2nd

two leaders emerged from the House of Basarab. Dan the 2nd was a worthy war general and a close aide to his uncle Mircea, who was the *voivode* of Wallachia. After Mircea died, he forcefully took the throne. Dan the 2nd's cousin, Radu the 2nd, was the son of the Mircea and he believed it was his right to be the next *voivode* of Wallachia. This was the beginning of the internal conflict within the Basarab House. Between 1420 and 1432, Dan took the title of *voivode* 5 times with support from the Ottomans and Bulgarian mercenaries. The first 4 times, he had been defeated by Radu who had the support of the *boyars*. Because of Dan's tendency to deal with the Ottomans, the orthodox *boyars* strongly opposed him. In 1427 A.D., Dan decisively defeated Radu and killed him. He then signed a peace treaty with the Ottomans.

This infighting led to the division of the House of Basarab into 2 lines: The House of Dănești and the House of Drăculești. The Dănești house included those whose claim to the throne was not according to lineage, but by the support of the *boyars*. The Drăculești house included those whose claim to the throne was according to lineage as they were the first descendants of Basarab the 1st. In 1436 A.D., the House of Drăculești, represented by Vlad the 2nd, comprehensively defeated the House of Dănești. Vlad the 2nd was known to be tactful and diplomatic with the Ottomans and Hungarians. Throughout his reign, he juggled the expectations of both. This included fighting alongside both armies at different times and paying tributes to each side as and when it seemed necessary.

A Romanian Boyar

As *voivode* of Wallachia, Vlad the 2nd formed favourable trade relations with the Transylvanian Saxons to the north. The Saxons were traders of a variety of goods. Acting as middlemen in the trade between the Levant and Central Europe, the merchants in Brăila, Târgoviste, Câmpulung, Bucuresti or Târgsor became involved in trading goods that were local or had been brought from beyond the Carpathians or the Black Sea. In Wallachia, raw materials were the goods of choice, and there were vast amounts of them: salt, cereals, livestock or animal products, skins, wax and honey. But economically, Wallachia was reeling because of the constant currency manipulation. The repeated monetary reform had rendered the local currency useless and of very little value. This was repeatedly done by the *boyars* in order to have favourable return on their land. But the other economic classes of the society were suffering heavily because their money's perceivable value kept changing.

Even though there was rebellion and in-fighting, Vlad the 2nd brought a measure of stability and peace to Wallachia. He was heavily criticised by the Byzantine Empire, when he agreed to pay a tribute to the Ottomans during the late 1430s A.D. His affiliation to the Order of the Dragon (a divine order created by the Pope to aggressively fight against those

John Hunyadi according to a 17th century artist

who opposed Christian rule) meant that he had to always fight against the Ottomans and never negotiate with them. But in order to maintain peaceful relations, he agreed to pay a yearly tribute to the empire and also handed over his 2 sons, Radu the 3rd and Vlad Tepes, into Ottoman custody. Summarily, the Byzantine Empire withdrew support for Vlad the 2nd and the Hungarian general John Hunyadi, an orthodox Christian, found his reason to go to war against Vlad. John Hunyadi was also bitter from his defeat at Vlad's hands while he was *voivode* of Transylvania.

In 1447 A.D., the in-fighting had reached its precipice. Vlad the 2nd was neither supported by the *boyars* nor the Christian clergy in Eastern Europe. The Hungarian empire, who wanted to regain control of the principality of Wallachia, conspired with the leader of the *boyars*, Vladislav the 2nd (Dănești) to overthrow Vlad the 2nd. The *boyars* were in agreement with the plan and John Hunyadi lead the attack on Wallachia. Vlad the 2nd lost the battle and was executed in a village in Targoviste. His eldest son Mircea the 2nd, was buried alive by the *boyars*. Vladislav the 2nd was installed as the new *voivode* of Wallachia.

During the same time, the Ottomans were preparing to lay siege to Constantinople, the heart of Byzantine Empire. To reach Constantinople, they had to take Wallachia and Transylvania. They had planned to use their relations with Vlad the 2nd when the time was right to move on Constantinople, but now the opportunity was gone. With the Christian crusader John Hunyadi and the puppet *voivode* Vladislav the 2nd in power, any support was highly unlikely.

In 1448 A.D., the principality of Wallachia became the most desired possession for the Ottomans, the Hungarians and the Romanians. Trade was growing, betrayal was expected and inconsequential battles were commonplace.

THE RISE AND RULE OF VLAD TEPES

MISSION: To become voivode of Wallachia and establish control over the independent principalities of Transylvania and Moldavia

At the age of 13, Vlad Tepes adopted his father's title of "Dracul" by pledging his allegiance to the holy mission of Christianity and the "Order of the Dragon". The word "Dracul" in Latin means Dragon. But in the Romanian language, it means "Devil". As Dracul's son, his title was Vlad Dracula. While his name has been the inspiration for Bram Stoker's legendary book, "Dracula", that is pretty much where the similarity between the two ends. Vlad Dracula was not restricted to the confines of his castle nor did he sleep in a casket, as is the tale of his fictitious namesake. Vlad Dracula was one of the most cunning negotiators and lethal generals in Romanian history.

THE 1ST REIGN, EXILE AND HIS ONLY MENTOR: PRINCE BOGDAN

Sometime in August, 1447 A.D., in Gallipoli, the first European stronghold of the expanding Ottoman Empire, Vlad Tepes was planning his escape from the confines of his Ottoman captors. He had been kept there against his will for 5 years. He wanted to escape and return to Wallachia to take his rightful place as voivode, succeeding his murdered father.

Sultan Murad the 2nd

Vlad Tepes was the rightful heir to the throne of Wallachia but he was not present there to claim his right. He had a choice to make now. Either he could scheme a daring escape from the Ottoman stronghold of Gallipoli or he could plan an attack and the resulting reclamation of his home, Wallachia. He couldn't do both. If he would escape from Gallipoli, he would be free of his bondage but would have to start fresh. With no allies or army, he would have to spend a long time recruiting an army strong enough to take hold of Wallachia from his cousin.

Vlad remembered that John Hunyadi was detested by the Ottomans. He had been a constant thorn in their side during their past incursions into Eastern Europe. The Ottomans had been so far unsuccessful in their attempts to enter Romania decisively because of the enigmatic Hungarian general. They had been repelled from the shared borders by a gritty defence, fuelled by an anti-Ottoman sentiment. But with the rightful prince by their side, the Ottomans could have a better chance than ever before. For Vlad, this was the chance to not just leave his Ottoman prison, but also to claim the throne that was his birth right.

POLITICAL CLIMATE OF THE PRINCIPLAITY OF WALLACHIA

Political State: Wallachia continued to be an absolute monarchy under Vlad the Impaler, like the generations before him

Geographical Extent: Wallachia was the southern-most extent of the 3 Danubian Principalities. Even though the geographic extent did not increase under his rule, Vlad maintain good relations (intermittently) with the leaders of the Transylvanian and Moldavian principalities

Local Aristocracy: When Vlad came into power, the *boyars* were the prominent aristocratic class of the Wallachians. By the end of his rule, they had either been purged or they had defected to Transylvania and Moldavia

Vassal Status: Till 1459 A.D., the suzerainty of the Ottoman Empire over Wallachia was accepted, even by leaders before Vlad. In 1459, Vlad rejected the Ottoman authority, especially because the remaining *boyars* favoured them.

Alliances: Vlad (along with John Hunyadi) had put an end to the infighting among the 3 principalities. They established favourable relations which continued till Vlad was dethroned in 1462.

After securing support from Sultan Murad the 2nd, better known as Mehmed the Conqueror, Vlad ascended to the throne of Wallachia in 1448 A.D. at the age of 18. It was an unprecedented that a boy of such a young age not only took the throne, but also secured support from a foreign empire. The *boyars* could not deny him his right and in October of 1448 A.D. and crowned him the new *voivode* of Wallachia. Vlad knew that his reign would not last. If Vladislav the 2nd wasn't killed in the battle against the Ottomans along the Danube, he would return and oust him from his throne. In fact, that is exactly what happened.

While fighting the Ottomans during the Battle of Kosovo, John Hunyadi and Vladislav received news of the return of Vlad Dracul's son, Vlad Tepes. Hunyadi ordered Vladislav to immediately turn back and take back Wallachia. As the Christians were being slaughtered, Vladislav made his way back to Wallachia. The attacks by Vladislav were relentless. The Ottomans saw this as a trivial pursuit as Vlad was still a teenager and even if they defeated Vladislav, another member of the Dănești house would oppose Vlad. The fighting within Wallachia would directly affect their attack on Constantinople. By late November, 1448, the Ottomans withdrew support and headed back. With no local support from the *boyars* (who favoured the Dănești line of the royal family, not the Drăculești line) and a non-existent military, in December, 1448, Vlad Tepes had been deposed and he had fled from Wallachia. This was his first lesson in political warfare. His lineage and army meant nothing if it was not supported by a strong alliance and a plan to purge those who had opposed him.

The betrayal by the Ottomans was another in the long list of betrayals that Vlad had faced since he was a child. To him, no one was a "man of their word" anymore. It had become a free for all. Those who had strong alliances would succeed. Those who would be honourable men would be swiftly executed. The cunning and adaptable would be celebrated. It was time for Vlad to adapt quickly. He could no longer harbour thoughts of a sustained rule.

From 1448 till 1456, Vlad remained in exile. Immediately after his deposition, he returned to the Ottoman Empire and took refuge in capital city of Edirne. It was here he realized that he no longer had the support of the Sultan Murad the 2nd. His plan to use them to establish himself in Wallachia had failed. In 1449, he moved to Moldavia where his maternal uncle, Bogdan the 2nd, had claimed the throne as voivode of Moldavia with the support of John Hunyadi. He stayed in Moldavia for the next 2 years, learning from his uncle. He learnt why his father had to break his oath to the Order of the Dragon to maintain his rule and peace in Wallachia. Prince Bogdan wanted Vlad to regain Wallachia, his birth right, but told him to remember that one victory won't get him the crown. He had to keep fighting, keep negotiating. It was an endless battle, till he would breath his last.

Prince Bogdan told him how Hunyadi had created a formidable reputation of a righteous Christian warrior who would stop at nothing in eliminating the enemies of the faith. That reputation allowed him to be victorious in battle as the opposition would shudder at the very thought of facing his legendary rage and wrath. Vlad listened intently and imbibed these lessons. He understood that a reputation follows one wherever one goes. Within the confines of the Danubian Principalities (Moldavia, Transylvania and Wallachia), a strong and memorable reputation would do more than any battle or incursion could.

ECONOMIC PROFILE OF THE PRINCIPALITY OF WALLACHIA

Primary Work: Trading goods from the East (Carapithian Mountains and the Black Sea) to the nations in Western Europe.

Major Goods: Salt, cereals, livestock or animal products, skins, wax and honey

Currency: Jurovalsar

Free and Fair Trade: Vlad ensured that there be free and fair trade across his empire. Even his relations with the Transylvanian Saxons was not the best, he still gave them the avenues to trade in Wallachia (albeit at only border fairs). Within Wallachia, after the removal of the boyar class, he urged the citizens to produce more and trade them to exporters.

Correction of currency manipulation: Before Vlad came into power, the Wallachian currency had been changed numerous times by the voivodes and the *boyars* in order reduce their debt. Vlad eradicated the constant currency manipulation by removing the right of the *boyars* in matters of monetary planning and policies.

Prince Bogdan also reinforced one lesson that he had learnt in the past as well. In the era when they lived, alliances were as ephemeral as rain in a desert. No alliance would last beyond the goals set for it. There was no scope for long term peace. Their realm had been torn by warring kings and princes for over a century. Now, the matter had become a family problem with the brothers and cousins willing to shed family blood to ascend to the throne, even if it is for as brief a period of time as a few months. There were no permanent alliances and whoever moves first, in all probability, wins.

For 2 years, Prince Bogdan's tutelage helped Vlad understand that he was far from prepared to begin a lifelong battle to acquire the principality of Wallachia. He studied under him, worked in different departments in his government and assisted in matters of militaristic and political relevance. In 1451, while attending a wedding, Prince Bogdan was assassinated by Peter Aaron, the bastard son of a previous *voivode* of Moldavia. Peter Aaron then ascended to the throne as *voivode* of Moldavia. Vlad, along with Bogdan's son Stephen the 3rd a.k.a. Stephen the Great, had to immediately leave Moldavia fearing their lives were in danger. Their fear was not unfounded. Peter Aaron ordered a search operation for them both immediately after Bogdan had been assassinated.

Both of them fled to Transylvania. In Transylvania, there was recognition of the Drăculești house and Vlad was given refuge. As both of them grieved the loss of a father and a mentor, Stephen suggested that they should seek the help of John Hunyadi, who was previously the joint *voivode* of Transylvania. An alliance with the Hungarians at this point would help both Vlad and Stephen. But Vlad had aligned himself to the Ottomans in the past and he hoped to present his previous stance as a necessity rather than a voluntary choice. Then, in November 1451, John Hunyadi himself concluded a 3 year truce with the Ottomans. It came as a surprise to

Vlad as he believed the iron-willed Hunyadi to be the most honourable of all Christians who would never negotiate with the Ottomans. It became clear to him that even Hunyadi could be broken if the ideal situation presented itself.

Vlad and Stephen remained together in their negotiation with Hunyadi and Vlad asked to be given refuge till he was ready to leave. Because of his declining relations with Vladislav the 2nd in Wallachia, he agreed to give him refuge in Transylvania but on his own terms. Vlad and Stephen were restricted to outskirts of the main cities of Transylvania. In 1452, he rejected Vlad's request to settle in Brasov and restricted all the *boyars* from giving Vlad shelter. Hunyadi wanted to subjugate Vlad to same kind of treatment as the Ottomans had done to him. He believed he could control Vlad and eventually rein him in as a puppet *voivode* of Wallachia. Little did he know, Vlad was happy to play along. It was all working to his benefit. He remembered the lesson from his first reign and the first lesson in political warfare: A strong alliance is the key to a successful overthrow.

WALLACHIA'S SOCIAL NORMS

End of Class Warfare: There was constant conflict between the boyars and the lesser economic classes of the Wallachian society. With the purging of the boyars, the class warfare was ended and Vlad made reforms that benefitted the working class.

Religion: Under Vlad, there was no acceptance of any other religion other than Christianity.

Monogamous society: There was zero tolerance for polygamy and adultery. In some cases, it was punishable by impalement.

Education: The education at the time was done by the Christian missionaries who would teach the young about the ways of Christianity and how their everyday lives should adhere to serving Christ.

By July 1456, Vlad had gained Hunyadi's trust and the Hungarian general entrusted the protection of the Transylvanian border in the hands of the future *voivode* against the advances of Vladislav the 2nd.

HIS 2ND AND LONGEST REIGN, "VLAD THE IMPALER" AND TAKING THE FIGHT TO THE OTTOMANS

In August, 1456, Vladislav the 2nd, *voivode* of Wallachia, moved on Transylvania and attacked the fortress of Făgăraș. In the process, he had razed a few villages of Saxonite people. Transylvania was the land of Saxons and this intensified the heightening tension between Vladislav and Hunyadi. At that time, Hunyadi was leading a Hungarian attack on Belgrade in the West. But if he didn't launch an immediate offence, Vladislav would have established control on many portions of the Principality of Transylvania. Hunyadi had to act and Vlad was awaiting orders. With a large army at his disposal, Vlad wanted to not just quell Vladislav's advances; he wanted to take back Wallachia decisively.

Vlad always had the survivor's instinct in him. He had learnt the art of deception and trickery in the field of battle very well. He divided his army into war parties and guerrilla units. The instruction to the warring parties was simple: seek and annihilate. The guerrilla units moved through the forests and reigned terror on the enemy. They poisoned the water, set traps and once the battalions were small enough, they'd attack them with fatal effect.

Within 2 weeks, Vlad's army had reached Wallachia. Once there, Vlad challenged his cousin, Vladislav to a bout of hand-to-hand combat. He wanted the bloodshed to stop. Vladislav accepted the challenge. Vlad defeated his

TECHNOLOGIAL ADVANCES BY THE PRINCIPALITY OF WALLACHIA

Weaponry: Steel armour, swords, spears and shields. There is not much evidence of use of war machines during Vlad's reign

Communication Methods: Letter writing and messengers. There was no organised or planned messenger system. This was an archaic method which was vulnerable to manipulation by enemies.

Architecture: The structures created during the reign of Vlad, including his own castles, town halls and barracks, employed modern methods of architectural design (like arches) and strong fortification methods to protect against attacks. In parts of modern Romania, Vlad is still called The Builder Prince of Wallachia.

cousin decisively. Following the bout, he killed Vladislav. With the support of the Hungarian empire, Vlad Tepes began his second and longest reign as *voivode* of Wallachia.

Immediately after taking the crown, Vlad sent a letter to the *Boghars* (local aristocracy) of Transylvania, notifying them of his ascension to the throne. In the same letter, he told them he would give them armed support in case of an attack by the Ottomans and he expected the same from them in case the Turks laid siege to Wallachia. The tone of the letter was not that of a request. He was simply notifying of his intentions as *voivode.* Vlad was not too fond of the *Boghars* as they had refused to shelter him when he was in Transylvania. He needed them on his side and he was in a position to dictate terms now. The *Boghars* assented to his request and accepted his rule.

Vlad had been planning his changes in Wallachia for more than 10 years now. He resented the *boyars* and the role they played in the execution of his father and his elder brother. He had held a grudge against them for a long time. Vlad ordered the purging of the *boyar* class. He ordered them to be rounded up for trial. Each of them was tried for treason against the Drăculești line of the Royal House of Basarab. More than a significant chunk of the *boyars* were found guilty and their punishment was Vlad's opportunity to do justice to the first lesson taught to him by his mentor: a formidable reputation will make your enemy think twice before moving against you.

The Act of Impalement

Impalement is an execution method where a large wooden spike is inserted in the rectum of a person and the wooden spike is erected, so that the spike slowly moves through the body, till it exits from the mouth (or another orifice). Vlad had all the guilty *boyars* impaled to set an example for the other citizens of Wallachia to remember. Soon after, he inflicted the same punishment on those *boyars* who had defected and were hiding in Transylvania. The word of this quickly spread across all the Danubian Provinces. Soon, Vlad Dracula became famous with another cognomen: Vlad the Impaler. The embellishments of his cruelty gave him a formidable reputation. Even foreign rulers became aware of the Wallachian *voivode* whose punishment for the living was worse than death.

In the West, the Hungarian army was returning from its successful annexation of Belgrade. A plague had engulfed the troops. During their arduous journey to reach home, John Hunyadi had fallen gravely ill. He died in his sleep. Vlad's long term ally Stephen the 3rd had taken the throne of Moldavia in the north. The younger son of John Hunyadi, Mattias Corvinus, had taken the throne in Hungary. Mattias supported Vlad's rule in Wallachia and believed him to be right ruler to repel (even attack) the Ottomans in the south.

In 1459 A.D., Vlad declared himself "lord and ruler over all of Wallachia, and the Transylvanian duchies of Amlaș and Fagaraș". This meant the Saxon traders of Transylvania had to adhere to the norms Vlad set down to continue their flourishing trade. By now, a feeling of fear of "Vlad the Impaler" had set in. The Saxons were infamous for their stories of Kings and their Kin. In their texts, they had described Vlad as a monstrous ruler who "drank the blood" of

A Portrait of Sultan Mehmed the 2nd by Italian Renaissance painter Paolo Veronese

"The Battle With Torches" by Romanian painter Theodor Aman

his victims while feasting every day. Vlad was feared and respected. Now, he was ready to take the fight to his oldest enemy: The Ottomans.

Sultan Mehmed the 2nd, the one Vlad wanted to kill since he was a teenage Ottoman prisoner, had ascended to the throne of the Ottomans. He was now their leader and in 1459 A.D. Vlad rejected the Ottoman Empire's suzerainty over the Principality of Wallachia. Vlad stopped paying the tribute to Mehmed. In addition, Vlad executed the envoys sent to him by Sultan Mehmed the 2nd. The nature of their execution was quite gruesome, where their turbans were nailed to their heads because they refused to take it off while in conference with Vlad. Their bodies were sent back to the Sultan along with the letter officially rejecting his authority over Wallachia.

In order to prepare for an impending war, Vlad had to acquire some strategically important locations along the Danube River. The fortress of Giurgiu was one such location. Dressed like Turkish troops, Vlad led a small army to the fortress, the only Turkish stronghold on the Romanian side of the Danube River. Once there, he spoke in fluent Turkish, tricking the soldiers to open the gates. Once inside, they quickly overthrew the Turkish contingent and took over the fortress. From there, he entered the Ottoman Empire and massacred the villages on the border. When he informed Mattias Corvinus of his plan of action, the Hungarian King asked him to cease and return to Wallachia. He also suggested keeping the peace with the Ottomans because the fall of Constantinople had cost the Roman Empire a lot of their monetary reserves and they could not afford another war. But Vlad was confident of his tactics and he had a plan to strike at the heart of the Ottoman Empire without launching a full scale war. It was risky, but Vlad was used to it.

Sultan Mehmed the 2nd raised an army of 150,000 soldiers to fight to not just fight against Vlad but to decisively conquer Wallachia. Mehmed planned to install Radu the Handsome, Vlad's younger brother who had been in Ottoman captivity since he was a child, as *voivode* of Wallachia. He began his march across the Danube and they landed at the Wallachian port of Brăila in 1462. They proceeded westward towards Targoviste, the capital of Wallachia. Vlad knew that he was heavily outnumbered and there was no help coming from Mattias Corvinus or Stephen of Moldavia. He relied on his old tricks again.

Vlad's troops destroyed paths, poisoned the water, burnt trees and killed livestock to leave nothing for the Ottomans to use during their march to Targoviste. Then, Vlad and his troops (dressed like Turks) entered the Ottoman camp with the intention of killing the Sultan. But instead of the Sultan's tent, they entered the tent of his Viziers and killed them instead. They fled from the site immediately and caused immense confusion among the army. Turks began to kill other Turks in the confusion, suspecting certain soldiers to be imposters. Within a few hours, 15,000 troops had been massacred. Vlad and his men escaped unscathed. The Sultan was enraged and he wanted to dispose of Vlad as soon as possible. He ordered the troops to begin their final march towards Targoviste. What they encountered on the march was so shocking that the Sultan turned back and headed to Constantinople in shock and awe of what he had witnessed.

Vlad retreated from Targoviste and while retreating, he left a monument for the Ottomans. When the Sultan's army entered Targoviste, they found a burnt town and a forest of the impaled. It had bodies of men, women and children of Turkic and Islamic Bulgarian descent. According the Laonikos Chalkokondyles, historian of the Ottomans, this is the description he gave of what was seen:

"The sultan's army entered into the area of the impalements, which was seventeen stades (1 stade is 600 feet) long and seven stades wide. There were large stakes there on which, as it was said, about twenty thousand men, women, and children had been spitted, quite a sight for the Turks and the sultan himself. The sultan was seized with amazement and said that it was not possible to deprive of his country a man who had done such great deeds, who had such a diabolical understanding of how to govern his realm and its people. And he said that a man who had done such things was worth much. The rest of the Turks were dumbfounded when they saw the multitude of men on the stakes. There were infants too affixed to their mothers on the stakes, and birds had made their nests in their entrails."

A Forest of the Impaled

Following this, the Ottomans suffered greatly in the summer heat of Wallachia. The water was not drinkable. Wild animals and fruits were charred. The endless forests and confusing trails made it impossible to know where Vlad was hiding. The Sultan turned back and headed towards Constantinople. Before leaving, he installed Radu as the *voivode* of Wallachia and instructed him that the next time he sees Vlad, it should be his cold, lifeless body. Radu established favourable relations with the remaining Wallachian *boyars* and the Transylvanian Saxons to return the region to peace.

Vlad in the meanwhile had fled to Transylvania and held negotiations with Mattias Corvinus on how to overthrow Radu and push the Ottomans back. It was here that he found out that the Pope had actually given ample funds for Vlad to fight against the Ottomans as well as permission to recruit Bulgarian and Austrian mercenaries. But Mattias Corvinus had spent the money on his own people without asking the Pope. If Vlad would report this to the Pope, Mattias would have to stand trial during which, in all likelihood, he would be found guilty. But Vlad could not do this while he while he was still negotiating with Mattias. Vlad tried to escape but he was apprehended.

To provide an explanation for Vlad's imprisonment to the Pope and the Venetians (the ones who sent the money for the war against the Ottomans), Corvinus presented three letters, allegedly written by Vlad, to Mehmed II, Mahemd's *vizier* Mahmud Pasha, and Stephen of Moldavia. According to the letters, Vlad offered to join his forces with the sultan's army against Hungary if the sultan restored him to his throne. These documents were forged to give grounds for Vlad's imprisonment and to cover up the unlawful spending of the war booty.

Vlad's imprisonment in Belgrade and the ascension of Radu the Handsome to the throne marked the end of Vlad's second rule as *voivode* of Wallachia. Till, 1475, he remained in prison.

STRENGTH-WEAKNESS-OPPORTUNITY-THREAT (SWOT) ANALYSIS OF VLAD TEPES

STRENGTHS	WEAKNESSES
"Vlad the Impaler": This was the cognomen given to Vlad by his enemies and was his most influential strength. The name was given because the large number of people he had impaled, regardless of title, gender and origin. **Headstrong:** From a young age, Vlad Tepes was a headstrong person who was clear about what he wanted. This facet of his played a considerable part in maintaining a diminutive yet high performing group of soldiers. **Authoritative:** Once in a position to command, he had the personality to get the best out of his troops. Even in matters of diplomacy, Vlad was always authoritative in his decision making **Strategist:** Vlad was an intelligent strategist from a young age, evident from his moves to escape from captivity and how he repeatedly negotiated favourable terms with those who had opposed and attacked him in the past. Apart from negotiation, Vlad was highly skilled as military tactician as well.	**Barbaric Rage:** Vlad never practiced diplomacy and restraint in dealing with his intended victims and prisoners. Probably stemming from abandonment issues from his childhood, Vlad's ungodly treatment of his victims gained him a terrible reputation. **God Complex:** Vlad suffered from a severe God complex that directed his actions and decisions in terms of diplomacy. **Glory Hunter:** As the son of a Prince, he sought to attain the glory that his father and grandfather had achieved. Because of that, instead of establishing an empire, he only desired short term victories.
OPPORTUNITIES	**THREATS**
Re-establish the Basarab House: With the execution of his father, Vlad and his younger brother, Radu, were the last surviving legitimate members of the Basarab house. By retaking Wallachia and establishing his rule in Romania, Vlad had the opportunity to restoring the Basarab house to its former glory. **Ending the Ottoman advance towards Constantinople:** The Eastern Roman Empire was fragmenting and Wallachia was key to ensuring the Ottoman advance towards the capital, Constantinople. By establishing himself in Wallachia, Vlad had the opportunity of stopping the advance of the Ottomans and be hailed as a saviour of the Romanian people. **Unite Wallachia, Moldova and Transylvania:** Even they were neighbouring each other, the 3 Romanian regions were non-cooperative, each ruling as an independent principality. By uniting the 3, Vlad had the opportunity to bringing together the people of the 3 principalities under a common cause.	**John Hunyadi, followed by Mattias Corvinus:** The Hungarian General, followed by his son Mattias Corvinus, had systematically worked to weaken Vlad's reign whenever they could. Throughout his time as *voivode,* Vlad's plans and campaigns would, in one way or another, be threatened by the 2 Hungarian father and son duo. **The Ottoman Empire:** For Vlad, the Ottoman Empire represented his forever nemesis. After his first reign as *voivode* of Wallachia, till his death, the Ottomans would try to shackle, depose or assassinate him not just because they wanted to control Wallachia, but also because of their deep seeded inherent hatred for his extreme methods. **His own cult of personality:** Because of his barbaric methods of execution and reprimanding prisoners, Vlad's reputation was that of an uncontrollable mad man who had to be deposed without mercy. This reputation of his made him paranoid about almost everyone who ever came in contact with him.

WHY IS VLAD THE IMPALER A TRANSACTIONAL LEADER?

Vlad Tepes ruled for a total of almost 10 years in Wallachia and Transylvania. While in comparison to many other leaders, it may seem like a short rule but it is important to consider the various characteristics of the times during which he ruled.

Imagine a world in the midst of centuries-long battles fought on the basis of faith, territory, lust and politics. Imagine a world where kings openly indulged in political betrayal (to establish "first mover advantage") and public executions (to establish "authoritarian rule"). As a ruler, each agreement could, for all practical purposes, be treated as temporary and always voidable. Blood relations and family ties was no protection against infighting and family feuds. Leaders (kings, princes and generals) had to constantly adopt new and innovative methods (both militaristic objectives and for governance) to repel or subdue the enemy as well as extend the duration of their rule as much as possible.

During such times, a leader was expected to have a royal lineage to support his claim to the throne. A ruler was also expected to have a large army to constantly fight for them. Continued worship of a faith that had been followed by the past generations of a ruler was one of the most important determinants of the support they would receive from their subjects. All these together would determine how successful a ruler would be during the medieval times in Eastern European region of Romania, Hungary and Bulgaria.

Vlad Tepes had none of these. His lineage (The Royal House of Basarab) had become fragmented. He had no support from the remaining members of his family. He had no long standing generals or an army that lasted longer than one or two battles. His pledge to be a devout Christian had always been under heavy scrutiny because of his initial alliance with the Ottomans, who were guided by the faith of Islam. Vlad would be ousted from his own home multiple times for many different reasons. But each time, he returned and reclaimed his throne.

Vlad's basic negotiation and alliancing technique was "The enemy of my enemy is my friend". Throughout his reign(s), he followed this practice in the many battles he had to fight. He had formed alliances with the Ottoman Turks, the Eastern Roman Empire, the Balkan rulers, the Saxons and the Hungarians, as and when it was required. His alliance would thoroughly depend on the situation that he found himself in. His cunning military techniques and uninhibited approach to battle sent a shiver down the spine of all his foes when they went to battle against him. He used guerrilla warfare, 'scorched earth' technique and ambush methods to such great effect that armies (far larger than his own) would break down under chaos and confusion. It is also said that Vlad's speeches to his troops were nothing short of a motivational master class. Even though, they would be heavily outnumbered in battle, they'd follow his instructions flawlessly. After each battle, he would allow his troops to freely take whatever they could carry and it would be their undisputed possession. This was a tactic of the Ottomans. Christian crusaders were not allowed to loot or plunder any battle ground or its occupants. But under Vlad, all his soldiers were allowed to do so.

As long as he was in power, he garnered support from his subjects by removing the *boyars*' privileges and spreading wealth and gains equally among all members of his Kingdom. Till today, even though he committed grave human rights violations, he is considered a heroic figure in many parts of Romania, for his bravery and fair treatment of his subjects.

His negotiation and militaristic intelligence, coupled with his barbaric, monstrous reputation of being "Vlad the Impaler", made him one of the most lethal yet successful leaders of the

Middle Ages. His reign brought with it the building of grand structures, betterment in trade and economic conditions and the repeated repulsion of the Ottoman Empire from entering Romania and Eastern Europe.

VLAD THE IMPALER'S DEATH

In November 1476 A.D., Vlad began his 3rd and shortest reign as the *voivode* of Wallachia. Mattias Corvinus, the Hungarian King, had recognized Vlad as the rightful prince of Wallachia. After ousting the Ottoman supported *voivode* Basarab Laiota from Wallachia, Vlad opened the doors of Wallachia to the aristocracy of Transylvania to trade with the merchants of Wallachia. He wanted to continue growing the trade of Wallachia, as he had previously done during his second reign.

By December 1476, Basarab Laiota returned to Wallachia with a large contingent of Ottoman troops. During the defence of Wallachia, Vlad was killed. He was decapitated and his head was sent to Sultan Mehmed in Constantinople to confirm his death.

VLAD THE IMPALER'S LAST KNOWN LOCATION

The place of his burial is unknown. According to popular tradition, Vlad was buried in a known monastery in Wallachia. However, the excavations carried out in 1933 found no tomb below the supposed "unmarked tombstone" of Vlad in the monastery church. According to another tale, his body was dismembered and sent to Sultan Mehmed the 2nd when he died.

VLAD THE IMPALER'S KILL COUNT

Vlad was known for his brutality and the tales of his mass killings became famous horror stories in all of Europe. It is estimated that he had impaled almost 100,000 of his own Wallachian people, most of them being *boyars*. In sacking of the outlying towns of Transylvania, the men, women and children he had killed stands at almost 30,000. During his attack on the Ottoman Empire, it is estimated that he killed 25,000 Turkish troops in the fortress of Giurgiu and the Ottoman villages near the Danube River. Another 20,000 Bulgarian and Turkic muslims had been killed in Targoviste when the Ottoman troops were advancing on capturing the capital. In total, according to historical estimates, Vlad's kill count ranges between 250,000 to 300,000.

STRATEGIC LEADERSHIP

IVAN VASILYEVICH: THE FATHER OF MODERN RUSSIA

"Success is 20% skills and 80% strategy. You might know how to succeed, but more importantly, what's your plan to succeed?"

- Jim Rohn

IVAN VASILYEVICH A.K.A. IVAN THE TERRIBLE

1530 A.D. – 1584 A.D.

GRAND PRINCE OF MOSCOW: 1533 A.D. TO 1547 A.D.

TSAR OF ALL RUS': 1547 A.D. TO 1584 A.D.

In the year 1450, in Germany, Johannes Guttenberg and another known simply as the "Master of Playing Cards" had commercialized the use of the world's first printer with movable type. That is, the same machine could be used to replicate different text types. The movable type page setting and printing using a press was faster and more durable. Also, the metal type pieces were sturdier and the lettering more uniform, leading to efficient replication of typography and fonts. They had begun with religious texts and soon had expanded to the printing of researched texts. While the "Master of Playing Cards" receded into the same obscurity he rose from, Gutenberg wanted to capitalize on his creation. Even though it had been a remarkable breakthrough, Gutenberg faced many financial and legal issues, stemming from the loans he had taken to complete his creation. Like many inventors and artists, his invention's full potential would be realized in the decades that followed his demise. Gutenberg lived on a stipend in his last days in Mainz and died in 1468.

A century later, in the expanding Rus' empire, the young Tsar of all Rus' Ivan Vasilyevich was made aware of Johannes Guttenberg and his work. The conversation stemmed from a discussion about how to spread the influence of Christian Orthodoxy in the empire and the new territories that were coming under their control including Kazan and the soon-to-be-conquered Astrakhan. Ivan knew that if he sent Christian emissaries to these places, they would only stir a rebellion from the people who had been under the rule of the Mongols and Golden Horde. They were people of multiple faiths and could not be converted with force. They had to contemplate and convert willingly.

Instead of sending priests, he wanted to send repeated messages (like a repeated announcement) of the deeds of Christ and the great humane benefits of following the noble path laid down by the son of God. Through written texts, it would serve like printed commandments that the people could read and follow. Once he learned about Guttenberg's invention, he knew this could be the tool to facilitate his mission. But Guttenberg had passed away long ago and his technology had been locked away because of the legal battles he had faced in the penultimate years of his life.

Pyotr Mstislavets was a Belarusian printer who had knowledge of the working of the movable type printing. The source of his knowledge is unknown but he had basic knowledge of how a similar machine to Guttenberg's could be assembled. Ivan Fyodorov had studied in Poland and maybe this was the time he met Pyotr. Fyodorov knew of Pyotr's knowledge of printing and specifically of movable type printing. With the recommendation of the church, Fyodorov approached the Tsar and offered to start the printing press he desired. The Tsar gave him chance to prove his ability.

In 1563, with the publication of the first text called Apostolos, the Moscow Print Yard was established as the first printing press of Rus'. The text was circulated across the empire and soon, the Tsar's vision was slowly taking form. It had cut down the production time significantly. This was a great threat to the traditional scribe community, who had been the recognised makers of replicas of a text till then. It drew their ire and that of their investors, the Boyars. They presented their grievance to the Tsar. The Tsar rejected their concerns and asked them to adapt to the modern methods if they wanted remain relevant and secure printing work contracts.

Sometime during the early 1560s, the scribe community had become very frustrated with the monopoly of the Moscow Print Yard. At the risk of drawing the ire of the Tsar, the workshop became the target of an arson attack. The whole workshop was burned to the ground. Pyotr and Fyodorov had received numerous death threats and this attack spelt the final straw. With the permission of the Tsar, they left Rus' because they no longer felt like they could be protected by the Tsar. After the attack and the departure of the printers, the Moscow Print Yard was shut down indefinitely. The scribe community re-established their monopoly.

Tsar Ivan Vasilyevich's attempt at establish a new technology had been thwarted by his own people. The Boyars of Rus', the local aristocracy, had been an annoyance for the Tsar for a long time. They were the middlemen who were draining the state's tax revenue in almost every field of work in Rus'. They practiced their authority and sometimes, even disregarded the orders of the Tsar. This defiance was stemming from the benevolent nature of Tsar Ivan's father, Vasili the Adequete. They were the investors in the scribe community as well and the popular rumour was that they had orchestrated this attack on the Moscow Print Yard. Tsar Vlad's existing annoyance with the Boyars now escalated to hatred. They had halted his vision of establishing a Christian Orthodox empire and if he had to get it going again, he had to solicit the services of the Boyar-led scribe community. The Tsar had no intention of dealing with the Boyars like his father had. They would not let them undermine his authority. For the first time, Tsar Vlad had the opportunity to make his intentions about the Boyars and their insolence absolutely clear.

The Tsar ordered the restart of the Moscow Print Yard under new management of Andronik Timofeevich Nevezha and his son. While the reparations in the printing press were being made, he ordered the execution of the Boyars who had a vested interest in the scribe community. This order was not even classified. It became open news that the Boyars were being hunted down. By the time the purge was complete, the Moscow Print Yard was in full swing again.

Tsar Ivan envisioned a society where everything would be state owned. According to him, this vision was equivalent to the will of God and it was his divine duty to execute it. He believed his authority to have been bestowed with God himself. He believed strongly that whatever he did was ordained by the almighty and was for the good of his people. This included the repression of any authority that was bringing any perceived injustice on his followers. Like the Boyars, many others would feel the brunt of his judgment when they interfered or questioned his vision or authority.

THE COUNTRY OF RUS' BEFORE IVAN THE TERRIBLE

At the turn of the 16th century, Rus' (Russia) was ruled by Ivan the 3rd, the Grand Prince of Moscow. Under his rule, the extent of land under the Rus' empire had expanded to 3 times of what it was when he had taken over. The land of his ancestors, Novgorod, had been one of his first major conquests. Many other lands had been acquired during and the Mongol threat had been neutralized. The Golden Horde had been decisively repelled from the Rus' lands. Because of these achievements, he was better known as Ivan the Great and his ruling era was called 'The Gathering of Russian Lands'. Russia's first expedition to the arctic was undertaken under the command of Ivan the Great.

Ivan the 3rd portrait from A. Thenet, La Cosmographie universelle, Paris, 1575

Another one of Ivan the Great's great achievements was the change in the identity of the Russian government. The government took on a much more autocratic form. This

The Seal of the Third Rome under Ivan the 3rd

resulted from the direct dominance of Moscow over the other cities and towns under the Rus' Empire. As Grand prince of Moscow, Ivan the Great exercised his authority over all the other nobility of belonging to the Rurik blood line. Since 1325, after the fall of Constantinople, Christianity found a home in the Rus' Empire with the Grand Princes of Moscow styled as the new ambassadors of the Christian faith. Living in this image, Ivan the Great, in his capacity as the Grand Prince of Moscow, exercised great control and repression on the other princes' of Rus'. He centralized the power to rule in his hands and it would continue to be so till the end of the Rurik Dynasty. During his reign, Moscow came to be referred to by spokesmen as the 'Third Rome'.

Ivan the Great died in 1505 and was succeeded by his eldest son from his second wife. His name was Vasili the 3rd. His reign was not as eventful as his father's. In fact, during his reign there was barely any expansion of the empire. His rule was characterized by the consolidation of power in the regions acquired by his father and the church-supported expulsion and execution of those who questioned his policies and decisions. It was a time of relative peace. But the economy was struggling. Vasili had inherited a Kingdom that was slowly shifting towards ruin. Because of the *boyars*, the collection of tax was not as voluminous as was expected. Apart from that, land ownership was predominantly in the hands of the *boyars*, the local land owning aristocracy. In a change of his father's policy, Vasili systematically increased land owned by peasants and farmers. When the *boyars* rebelled, Vasili punished them by reducing the immunities and privileges afforded to them.

An engraving of Vasili the 3rd by a contemporary European artist

In a way, Vasili's treatment of the *boyars* became the inspiration for his son's, Ivan the 4th, eventual wrath against them. Vasili had realized, as did Ivan, that the local aristocracy were throttling the country's economy and they had no intention of investing their gains either to improve the state of the peasants who worked under them or to the State to support the Grand Prince. Thus, their extreme actions towards the *boyars* became a direct consequence of this act of collective frugality.

Vasili was child-less till the age of 54. In order to make sure that his own heir would ascend to the throne of Grand Prince of Moscow and as the Tsar of all Rus', Vasili had forbidden his brothers from having a male child till he had son of his own. Vasili's wife, Solomonia Suborova, had been married to him for over 20 years but had been barren. As Vasili grew older, the rumours about his impotence began to surface and he took a drastic step. Going against Christian practices, Vasili divorced Solomonia and married a younger Siberian princess named Elena Glinskaya. Elena was only 16 years old when she married Vasili. 7 years later, an heir was conceived named Ivan the 4th. Ivan had a younger brother too. He was named Yuri. He was born deaf.

In 1533, Vasili died. He had been mockingly named Vasili the Adequate, because he did just enough to maintain the status quo of the Rus' empire. When he died, Ivan was only 3 years old. On his death bed, Vasili had instructed his young wife, Elena, to rule till Ivan came of age. Elena ruled as Grand Princess Consort of Moscow for 5 years after Vasili's death. She managed good relations with the *boyars* and handled matters of war with relative maturity. She also introduced a new unified monetary system in a bid to reduce the burden of debt on the economy. She signed an armistice with Lithuania, while taking over Sweden. But even after achieving all of this, Moscow was rife with rumours about her relationship with a young Boyar who was a scheming socialite. Elena taught Ivan the importance of being of well-read and understanding theology as a future ruler of Rus'. She wanted her son to be prepared.

Rus' under the rule of Ivan the 3rd and Vasili the 3rd

To have a Grand Princess ruling Moscow was something that hurt the sentiment of traditionalists and they wanted her to be usurped or assassinated. This sentiment was strong among the *boyars* as they saw this as an opportunity to take the throne of Rus' for themselves. Among them, a family named the Shuisky's were the one who are the prime suspects of Elena's assassination. Because of the lack of evidence, it can only be speculated that she was killed by poison. It is believed that it was the governess of her eldest son who had poisoned her. After her death, the *boyars* fought for power for 8 years. The new monetary system was repealed and the *boyars* borrowed illegitimately from the state. The economic conditions were going from bad to worse. Without anyone of authority to reprimand them, the *boyars* literally did whatever they wanted to. Elsewhere, the fragmented Khanates of the erstwhile Mongol Empire and the Golden Horde were consolidating power with the intention of striking Moscow, taking back power and ending the rule of the nobility in Rus'.

THE COUNTRY OF RUS' UNDER THE RULE OF IVAN THE TERRIBLE

MISSION: To establish himself as the 'Tsar of all Rus' with the image of "divine and absolute power"

After his mother's assassination in 1538, Ivan lived a life in obscurity. He closely observed the constant struggle for power that ensued between the powerful Boyar families of Moscow. He learned his lessons in theology, from the arch bishop of Moscow, Makarius. In 1541, arch bishop Makarius had finished the first edition of the "Great Menaion Reader", the definitive compilation of all Russian saints and their deeds. Soon after this, Makarius also wrote the "Book of Degrees of Royal Geneology" which chronicled the lineage of Ivan. Ivan read these books with great interest and learnt of the rulers of his own family. When they discussed these texts, at some point during their conversations, Makarius encouraged Ivan's desire to establish a Christian state based on the principles of justice, once he came to power. The Arch Bishop groomed Ivan while systematically consolidating his own position as one of the most influential Bishops across all of Rus' through his research and writings. With him by his

Makarius, Archbishop of Moscow

side, Ivan became sure of the Church's support for his rule, something that none of the *boyars* had.

Ivan exchanged letters with his brother Yuri, who was in the small principality of Uglich, keeping his spirits up, even though they were being ill-treated because of their father's deeds and animosity of the *boyars*. Ivan assured him that the day would come when they would free of their suffering and with the support of the Church, they would take back their rightful place at the top. For 9 years, Ivan and his trusted circle of people were able to keep the power-hungry *boyars* at bay till he came of age to execute his detailed vision.

In January, 1547, Ivan was crowned the 'Tsar of all Rus" with the blessing of Makarius and the church. Ivan the Great, Ivan's grandfather, had previously used the title Tsar in his communications during his reign. But he had never been officially christened with the title. Ivan was the first Russian ruler to be officially given the title of "Tsar of all Rus"'. His authority was undisputed and during his first half of his reign, Ivan ruled like he had been trained.

1547-1560: THE FIRE IN MOSCOW, THE FIRST RUS' PARLIAMENT AND THE END OF THE MONGOLS

In June 1547, a few months after the coronation and subsequent wedding of Tsar Ivan, Moscow witnessed one of the worst tragedies in Russia's history. In June, a fire broke out in the city that destroyed a large part of the city. The fire also reached the Kremlin towers which were storehouses for gun powder. This resulted in major explosions and the fire spreading even more. The damage had displaced 80,000 people and killed 2,700 to 3,700 people (not including children). The damage brought widespread poverty to the city. The people lost their homes as well as their means of earning a living.

Immediately after the fire ceased, the populace of Moscow pointed the finger of blame towards the maternal side of Tsar Ivan's family. Led by the *boyars*, they accused Tsar Ivan's grandmother and uncle of using witchcraft to spread the fire in Moscow. This led to the stoning and death of Ivan's maternal uncle, Yuri Glinski. He was killed in front of the arch bishop Makarius in the Cathedral of the Dormition. The extended Glinski family in Moscow were hunted down. Eventually, the mob came calling for the Tsar's grandmother but he refused to hand her over. He stood strong on his stance and eventually the mob eased off.

Tsar Ivan's stand on the matter served 2 purposes at the same time. Not only had he declared himself as the supreme authority in Moscow, but with the purging of the Glinski family, many pretenders to the throne had also been executed. After the noise around the fire had been quelled, Ivan wanted to establish his military might on the Tatar Mongols in Kazan. He knew they had been planning an offensive against him for some time. The young Tsar did not have to worry about an uprising against him because Makarius would remain in Moscow to rule in his stead. As a Saint of the Christian order, Makarius was as good as untouchable. In 1547, Tsar Ivan led the first strike against Kazan. It was unsuccessful. He tried again in 1549. He was struck down yet again by the resilient Mongols.

When he returned to Moscow, Makarius advised him

POLITICAL CLIMATE OF THE RUSSIAN EMPIRE

Political State: Rus came under the power of the imperial class, with Ivan the 3rd founding the rightful heir of the Rurik dynasty.

Geographical Extent: By the end of the rule of Ivan the 4th, the Rus empire stretched from the Baltic Sea to the middle of the Central Asian Steppe, spanning almost 4.5 million square miles.

The Boyar Class: The Boyar class were the local land owning aristocracy who would exercise control intermittently on Moscow.

The End of the Mongols: Even though the Mongol Khanates had been all but conquered, the conquest of Kazan, Astrakhan and Siberia had left some fragmented Mongols who tried numerous unsuccessful incursions into Rus. By the end of Ivan the 4th's rule, they had been conquered.

The Tsar was only accountable to God: After his ascension to the unprecedented position of Tsar of all Rus, Ivan made it clear that he was accountable to no man for his decisions. He spread Christian orthodoxy and became a figure of worship among his subjects.

to focus his attention on domestic matters. This included updating archaic laws and allowing the *boyars* to represent their interests to the Tsar in a civilized manner. Together they went about creating the Sudebnik of 1550. The Sudebnik was the body of laws and policies that had been created by Ivan the Great in 1497. Tsar Ivan believed that things had changed since the rule of his grandfather and he introduced changes that would usher in a new era in Moscow and all of Rus'. The Sudebnik of 1550 liquidated the judicial privileges of the *boyars* and strengthened the role of state judicial bodies. There was better representation of local communities in legal proceedings. Town and rural communities had the right to self-management and the distribution of taxes. The Sudebnik confirmed the right of peasants to leave their feudal lords. The law precisely defined that the peasant had the right to leave the landowner after the payment of two fixed fees (a "break-away" fee called pozhiloye and a transportation fee called povoz). Because of the updated Sudebnik, Tsar Ivan won the public's favour.

Under the new Sudebnik, the first ever Russian Parliament was also convened. It was called Zemsky Sobor. This parliament consisted of representatives of the nobility, church and the common people. The first such parliament was held in 1549. These parliaments were meant to resolve matters of a legislative

ECONOMIC PROFILE OF THE RUSSIAN EMPIRE

Primary Work: Russia was an agrarian economy under Ivan's rule and the primary work Russians undertook was farming and animal husbandry.

Transnational Trading: Throughout his reign, he repeatedly established trade relations with nations in the West including England, Livonia (now Lithuania and Estonia) and many other countries.

The Beginning of Russian Serfdom: Through the strict peasant movement laws introduced under Ivan's regime, the foundation for Russian serfdom had been laid. Because of this, there were numerous famines and droughts during and after Ivan's reign.

War was periodical: Another telling feature of Ivan's rule was his propensity to declare war on neighbouring nations in an attempt to acquire more land and increase the size of the Rus' empire. This resulted in the Russo-Turkish war, Livonian War, the Crimean raids and Siberian War.

Currency: Roubles

nature. This was the first time in Russian history that a platform was given to representatives of all strata's of Russian society to be involved in decisions about the state. Even though the economy was in severe depression, the outlook during these first few years of Tsar Ivan's reign was characterised by a growing hope of a positive future. Not only were his policies progressive, but they were also meant to create an inclusive society and reduce the influence of the local aristocracy.

In 1552, with matters on the domestic front resolved, Tsar Ivan turned his attention back towards Kazan because the man he had installed as the ruler of Kazan had been ousted. Shah Ali, a pro-Russian Mongol leader, had been ousted by the patriotic party's leader. Tsar Ivan led an army of 150,000 strong to Kazan with the intention of permanently assimilating it into the Russian Empire. After 2 months of fighting, Tsar Ivan finally conquered the Khanate of Kazan. After the victory, the Mongols dispersed into smaller guerrilla units. They were dealt with in the snow covered forests and outlying towns over the following 4 years.

The might of the Mongols had been dissolved and in 1556, the Khanate of Astrakhan, located at the mouth of the Volga River was taken by the Tsar's troops without fighting. They also destroyed the largest slave market along the Volga River. The remaining Mongols were prohibited from settling along rivers and in Russian cities. Their settlements in the specified zone were destroyed. This officially ended the influence of the Mongols in Russia. From that moment onward, the Volga became a Russian river, and the trade route to the Caspian Sea was rendered safe.

Tsar Ivan returned to Moscow to much fanfare and a hero's reception in 1556. For the next 2 years, Tsar Ivan consolidated his influence at home and worked on improving diplomatic relations with neighbouring nations. With both banks of the Volga now secured, Tsar Ivan prepared for a campaign to force an exit to the sea, a traditional concern of landlocked Russia. Trade with Europe depended on free access to the Baltic and this could only be done by having a decisive control over the country of Livonia (modern-day Latvia and Estonia). He got his opportunity in January 1558, when Livonia broke its truce with Russia. According to the truce, Livonia could not enter into an alliance with Poland-Lithuania. But Livonia had done exactly that in the Treaty of Pozvol. Tsar Ivan saw this as the perfect opportunity and invaded Livonia. But little did he know, this was a war that would last for the rest of his life.

1560-1580: ABDICATION, THE OPRICHNINA AND HIS UNDISPUTED MONARCHIC, IRON FIST RULE

The decade of 1560-70 brought a lot of unforeseen challenges for Tsar Ivan. The Livonian War had not proved to be a simple annexation of territory as he had thought. In April, 1560, one of Tsar Ivan's closest advisors, Prince Andrey Kurbsky, defected to Lithuania and led the charge against the Russians in Poland-Lithuania. This sowed the seeds for Tsar Ivan's increasing suspicion of nobility. Then, in August of 1560, Tsarista (wife of Tsar Ivan) Anastasia Romanovna died under mysterious circumstances. Tsar Ivan was distraught and the rumour that the *boyars* had poisoned the Tsarista added to Tsar Ivan's growing paranoia. Apart from the arch bishop Makarius, Tsar Ivan had lost faith in almost all of his close confidants. He began to tighten his grip on all governance and militaristic matters. If not through diplomatic governance, he would exercise control by instilling fear.

The Moscow Print Yard was ordered to continue printing texts about religion and the Tsar Ivan's divine right as their ruler. The edicts were meant to instil a God-like image of Tsar Ivan among the commoners and this worked to a large extent. Order was restored, Ivan had married again and the commoners were falling in line, respecting their ruler out of fear of the cost of defiance. Then, in early 1563, the arch bishop Makarius died. He was the most rational and trustworthy advisor to Tsar Ivan. After his death, Tsar Ivan wanted to establish an iron fist rule. Tsar Ivan's vision for Moscow had not changed. He wanted to gain as much land as possible and officially declare them as Russian lands. But for him to continue his conquests, he had to make sure that things on the domestic front were controlled.

Tsar Ivan wanted the Boyar class, because of the treasonous nature, to unequivocally submit to his will. The Boyar class was hated by the nobility and the commoners alike. In late 1564, Tsar Ivan abdicated his throne and left Moscow. In his absence, Moscow fell into chaos. The city's common people began hunting down the *boyars*. Fearing for their lives, the Boyar aristocracy sent an envoy to Ivan and begged him to return. Tsar Ivan agreed to return under one condition: He be given absolute monarchic control. That is, he could not be questioned nor could he be prosecuted for his actions. Believing him to be the lesser of two evils, the *boyars* agreed to his demand.

THE RUSSIAN EMPIRE'S SOCIAL NORMS

Religious Rigidity: Christian orthodoxy was the main religion and it was personally promoted by Ivan, in his propaganda and his actions. He wanted people to convert to Christian Orthodoxy, promising them protection in return.

***Boyars* were detested:** In his propaganda, Ivan had spread the word that the *boyars* were the enemy of the state and they were draining the earnings of the peasants.

Arts and artists were supported and promoted: Being a writer himself, Ivan had a great deal of appreciation for art and artists. They'd be given special treatment and protection from the Oprichnina, Ivan's personal army.

Meritocracy was practiced: In the military, Ivan reorganized the appointment methods. He made a method based on meritocracy and the achievements of the contenders.

Polygamy and adultery were punishable: As per the tenets of Christian Orthodoxy, polygamy, homosexuality and adultery were punishable by death across the empire.

Upon his return to the throne, Tsar Ivan created the Oprichnina, a state policy that resulted in mass repressions, public executions and confiscation of land and property from Russian aristocrats i.e. the Boyar class. The campaign included creation of a special army called the Oprichniki. From 1565 to 1572, the Oprichniki carried out the Tsar's orders for purging and confiscation of land of the aristocracy who were found guilty of embezzlement and treason. Soon enough, those who had begged for his return became the target of his wrath. In the Rus' parliament of 1566, the *boyars* requested the abolishing of the Oprichnina and to allow them to take back the lands that had been confiscated. The Tsar was not happy and his stand on the Oprichnina became even sterner because of the Boyar's history of deception. He denied their request.

The Moscow Print Yard had ended the monopoly of the Boyar-controlled scribe community. The efficient machines of the Print Yard had rendered the efforts of the traditional scribe community obsolete. As a way to send a message to the Tsar, the Moscow Print Yard was burned down, allegedly by the *boyars*. In retaliation, Tsar Ivan ordered the Oprichniki to purge of all *boyars* who had a vested interest in the scribe community. He offered work to the scribes in the restarted Moscow Print Yard and resulting freedom from the *boyars*. This further reduced the influence of the *boyars* in Moscow.

The Oprichniki's cruel and extreme methods became known across the empire. Systematically, by 1570, Tsar Ivan also eliminated all the claimants to the throne (his cousins and relatives of the Rurik Dynasty bloodline) with the last heir, Vladmir of Starista, being executed in 1569. This cleared the path for the undisputed rule of Tsar Ivan, with the support of the Holy Christian church. The closest claimant to his throne was his eldest son, Ivan Ivanovich, from his first marriage. His son accompanied Ivan and learned his methods. Ivan wanted to be a worthy successor to his father and be as well read as him.

From 1570 onwards, Tsar Ivan focussed his attention to foreign affairs. He made peace with the Ottoman Empire to the south. After the 1571 fire in Moscow that ravaged the city, he swore to eradicate the Crimean Tatars, who had started the fire. He ended the advance of last Crimean Tatars by decisively defeating them during the Battle of Molodi in 1572. The one war he still could not end was the Livonian War. It had now dragged on for over 10 years. It was clear that there could no longer be a peace agreement, as the opposition now consisted of Livonia, Poland-Lithuania and Sweden. From 1570-77, Tsar Ivan repeatedly attacked the Kingdom of Livonia but to no avail.

THE RUSSIAN EMPIRE'S TECHNOLOGICAL ADVANCES

Weaponry: Hand pishchals, cannons, howitzer and other barrel guns

The Moscow Print Yard: Ivan introduced Rus' to the science of printing with the establishment of the Moscow Print Yard. The printing press was instrumental to spreading Ivan's propaganda and sustaining his influence as a God-like figure amongst his people.

Wide usage of the Abacus: The abacus was used widely as a calculation tool in Rus.

Battery Towers: During Ivan's reign, many of the castles and fortified structures of Rus' had battery towers which were meant to be outlook posts as well as towers armed with canons to launch aerial assaults on the enemy.

To spread the war sentiment across his empire, Tsar Ivan ordered the Oprichniki to raid the city of Novgorod, the second largest city of Russia. In 1570, the *boyars* of Novgorod had decided to align itself to Lithuania and the Tsar did not take to this very kindly. In the raid, 60,000 people were massacred by the Oprichniki. It sent a chill down the spine of the nation collectively. The fear of the Tsar was as real as it could get. Even though famine and plague had hit the country, the citizenry were willing to fight for the Tsar in whatever capacity they could, to avoid being murdered by the Oprichniki.

By 1580, the conquest of Siberia was also complete, led by the Cossack leader Yermak Timofeyevich. When the Livonian war came to an end in 1583, Tsar Ivan had grown very tired by then. He was weary and slowly started to step away from the state matters. He presided over the parliaments and would communicate his decisions to the citizens of Moscow through his close entourage. He grew increasingly paranoid because of the repeated betrayals he had faced during his reign. During his final years, he made peace with Poland-Lithuania and released all Russian territories in Livonia back to Livonian control.

STRENGTH-WEAKNESS-OPPORTUNITY-THREAT (SWOT) ANALYSIS OF IVAN VASILYEVICH

STRENGTH	WEAKNESS
"Ivan Grozny/Ivan the Terrible": This was the cognomen given to him by his followers because of his extreme methods. **Royal lineage:** Ivan became the Grand Prince of Moscow at the age of 3. He consolidated power at the age of 17 when he was declared the "Tsar/Czar of all Rus". His royal lineage was instrumental in his protection against those who wanted to overthrow him. **Authoritarian:** Once Ivan realized his power could not be challenged, he became very stern in the implementation of his decisions. **Visionary:** Ivan envisioned a united Rus governed by strong leader chosen from Russian nobility with trade relations with nations across the globe.	**Paranoid:** Because of his upbringing and the abuse he faced at an early age, he suffered mild to severe bouts of paranoia. **Jealousy:** Ivan's jealousy was reflected in the number of wives he had. Many of them were sent to become nuns or killed when he suspected them of adultery. When his son questioned his ability as a military commander and offered himself to take command, Ivan killed him with own hands. **God complex:** Because of his status as a ruler from the age of 3, he became convinced of his divine status. He believed that his decisions as a ruler were confirmed by God and could not be questioned. When they were, he answered with great fury, as he believed was his right.
OPPORTUNITY	**THREATS**
End the line of the Khanates in the East: For Ivan to expand Rus to the East, he had to end the line of Tatar Mongols, who were scattered but still had khanates in different parts of the Central Asian Steppe. **Make Moscow the centre of his empire:** Being the Grand Prince of Moscow, he had envisioned the city as the centre of his eventual empire with the fortified Moscow Kremlin serving as the seat of his power **Establish favourable trade terms with the west:** Because he envisioned Rus' to be a trade friendly nation, he established trade relations with European nations in the West. **Invest in printing to spread propaganda:** After learning of the printing technology being developed in the far east, it became important to use the technology to spread his ideology throughout all of Rus'.	**Rebellion from t*he boyars:*** When he began prosecuting and purging them, he always risked a rebellion, across Rus', by the *boyars*. **The image of one who slaughtered those who opposed:** Many of his diplomatic relations with other nations was quite shifty because of his reputation of being a violent suppressor and his cognomen "Ivan the Terrible". **His own offspring:** Many times during his life, he had accused his own sons of having affairs with their own mothers. Word of this spread swiftly across the empire, becoming a point of ridicule and reducing his influence. **Fear of betrayal, stemming from paranoia:** During his later life, Ivan became convinced that his inner circle would betray him, even though there were no signs of the same. He began a systematic purging of officials who had never opposed him.

WHY IS IVAN VASILYEVICH A STRATEGIC LEADER?

A strategic leader is one whose actions are guided by a strategy that seems optimal to them to achieve one or many outcomes of the proposed chain of action. In this type of leadership, the strategic leader is also called the chief strategist. From an analytical perspective the chief strategist's job is to be the architect of the perfect strategy. Leaders holding this perspective see the strategy itself as the outcome and managing the process is delegated, frequently to individuals who lack line of sight to the senior person. In essence, a strategic leader aims to stay in power by adopting different strategies and practices to keep the ball rolling.

For Ivan the Terrible, the strategy he designed was an adoptive one that would cement his reputation as a 'divine and just ruler'. Ivan inherited the title of the Grand Prince of Moscow at the age of 3, as per the will of his father, Vasili the 3rd. However, he did not inherit his right to rule till he was 16 years old. Till he came of age, his ideology was moulded by many different influences. This included the final years of the Mongolian Golden Horde's aggressive influence on the Rus' society, the domestic battle for power between the Boyar families and the decaying Rus' economy. In his formative years, Ivan read voraciously about Christianity and the exploits of the past rulers of Rus', majorly his own family. He aligned himself to the archbishop Makarius who would ensure his safety and eventual ascension to a position of universal power.

At the age of 16, Ivan was crowned the Tsar of all Rus', making him the first ruler of his kind in the history of the empire with the blessing of the church. Up until this point, there had only been Grand Princes of the different major cities and stronghold of the Rus' empire. Ivan used his devoutness as an orthodox Christian, modelling himself as the one whom God had chosen and the coronation became

Russia under Ivan the Terrible in 1584

the right of passage to acquire his divine right as the ruler of his people. Almost immediately after ascending to the throne, Ivan began to spread the influence of Christianity across his empire. With the support of the church, he wanted to eradicate the influence of any other faith on his people and attain absolute control over them on a personal level.

Ivan also wanted to emulate the success of his grandfather, Ivan the Great, during his rule. Ivan the Great was hailed as a wise yet aggressive ruler who wanted to expand the horizon of the Rus' empire. He had successfully repelled the advances from the Mongolian Golden Horde and the Ottomans in the East. He had waged wars and been a successful commander of his troops. Ivan believed his grandfather's work had been left incomplete as his father was not interested in gaining more land, but to maintain harmonious conditions domestically. From the beginning of his reign, Ivan worked to end the line of the Tatar Mongols and later moved to continue expansion in Siberia, thus, expanding the Rus' empire to a size of 4.5 million square miles. This added to his reputation of being an ambitious ruler who wanted his country to prosper and be feared by their enemies.

Domestically, he envisioned the eradication of those who were standing in the way of centralized economic gains. To expand his empire, he had to wage wars constantly with neighbouring nations. For this, he required an unending war chest. The ones who were interfering with this were the *boyars*. From his teenage years, he had identified the *boyars* as the root cause for the great suffering of the Rus' economy. They were the designated middle men, because of their status as local aristocracy, who would eat into the gains of the farmers and other artisans because of their status as the local aristocracy. Ivan and the working class of the Rus' society were repulsed by the *boyars*; the latter suffered under their harsh working conditions and the unfair share of production they took from the peasants.

Ivan systematically removed the influence of the *boyars* through different measures, including executions, trials and change in policy. His actions against them won him popularity amongst the people. The people favoured his rule and the dismantling of the Boyar influence. Ivan managed to turn the people against them and the people believed in a better future, where they would be rid of the control by the *boyars*. He had done so to such an extent that when he abdicated in 1564, the *boyars* begged him to return as they feared a violent uprising from the peasants and the working class. When he did return, he was supposedly respected by the proletariat and deeply feared by the *boyars*, who had no choice but to adhere to his instructions of centralizing the economic gains from the agrarian activities.

By the end of his reign, he had gained the status of a divine ruler that he had envisioned for himself with the continued support from the church and its clergy. As a result, there were very few who opposed him and even fewer who would dare to rise up against him.

IVAN'S DEATH

During his last years, Ivan had become highly paranoid and feared betrayal from everyone who surrounded him. After he murdered the heir to the throne and his own son, Ivan Ivanovich, Tsar Ivan descended into a dark spiral. His chamber would always have boiling mercury, the usage of which he had become highly addicted to. It is said that he used the mercury as a pain killer for the severe headaches he suffered from. The validity of this claim can be debated.

From the heavy usage of the mercury, it is believed that Ivan suffered from severe mercury poisoning, thus explaining his increased delusion towards the end of his life. In March, 1584, he died of a stroke while playing chess with a close associate named Bogdan Belsky. His death was sudden and the state was unprepared for it.

Following his death, the Rus' empire fell into the hands of his incompetent middle son, Feodor, whose rule was marked by gross inefficiency, resulting in the end of the Rurik dynasty and the ushering in of 15 years of suffering better known as the "Times of Trouble".

IVAN'S LAST KNOWN LOCATION

Ivan was buried in the Cathedral of the Archangel in Moscow.

IVAN'S KILL COUNT

Ivan Vasilyevich got his cognomen "Ivan the Terrible" because of his reputation of savagery and barbarism while dealing with his enemies and conspirators. His execution style ranged from beheading, extreme torture and impalement. Under his command, the Oprichnina, his own personal army, committed mass killings as well as systematic purging of people who opposed or questioned the decisions made by him. By styling himself as the right hand of God, Ivan believed, without remorse, that killings were a necessary part of his job of executing the orders given by God. His final kill count is confirmed to range from 150,000 to 220,000 people, including men, women and children.

AUTOCRATIC LEADERSHIP

KING LEOPOLD THE 2ND: THE PRIVATE SECTOR VANDAL OF CONGO

"Men are moved by two levers only: fear and self-interest."

- Napoleon Bonaparte

KING LEOPOLD THE 2ND
(1835-1909)

DUKE OF BRABANT, PRINCE OF SAXE-COBURG
AND GOTHA, DUKE OF SAXONY
(1840-1865)

KING OF BELGIUM
(1865-1909)

SOVEREIGN OF THE CONGO FREE STATE
(1885-1908)

Henry Morton Stanley acted as Leopold's agent in his annexation of the Congo. Stanley was well versed with the Central African mainland and had navigated Africa twice before.

When Leopold approached Stanley initially, he refused. He did not wish to return to Africa then, and most importantly, he was not enamoured by the idea of being the face of a war for territory between the Europeans and Africans. But Leopold did not relent. He offered Stanley a great deal of money, estate and the chance to return to his home, England, after the expedition was over. Stanley finally agreed and led his collections of officers and soldiers to the land known as Congo.

Under the pretence of leading a missionary drive under the Belgian company called International African Association, Stanley oversaw the building outposts and roads in Congo to transport the extracted materials to the ports where they would be shipped to Belgium. He wanted to establish diplomatic terms with the local tribe chiefs and leaders, but Leopold was strictly against this. He wanted to show no mercy to the Congolese people and subjugate them to such harsh conditions that they would submit to his will.

Once Congo came under his control, Leopold wanted Stanley to proceed further eastwards into Zanzibar. Leopold was well aware of Stanley's good relations with Tippu Tib, the Arab slave trader whose legend was well travelled. Tippu Tib controlled the lands of almost all of East Africa and reigned down terror on those who opposed him. To conquer Zanzibar, Stanley had to go through Tippu Tib and challenge his thriving ivory trade. Stanley advised against this because the Belgian troops and the local Congolese soldiers were less, when compared to the might of Tippu Tib's army.

Tippu Tib was known for ravaging villages and extracting ivory. His prisoners and goods were sent all across the Middle

East via. the port of Zanzibar. He shared his gains with the Sultan of Zanzibar and in return, Tippu would be given free rein on all the natural resources of Zanzibar. Over time, he had consolidated his claim and established himself as one of the most powerful people in all of Eastern Africa.

Leopold and Stanley had to buy time, till their army was big enough to compete with Tippu Tib. Stanley negotiated an agreement with Tippu that if he would not attack Congo, he could source Ivory from certain parts of Congo and there would be peace between Zanzibar and Congo. As time went on, Leopold received strong support from other European powers for his claim on Congo. He even received military support from these nations. Stanley created a local army called the Force Publique, which included soldiers and mercenaries who would be willing to kill anyone for the right price.

Soon, Tippu Tib got wind of what Stanley and Leopold were scheming. He broke their agreement and began plundering the outer fringes of Congo for ivory and slaves. This gave Leopold the right to declare war on Tippu Tib. Till 1886, Tippu Tib had collected fields full of ivory from the fringes of Congo. The same year the fighting began. Though, the count of those killed was innumerable but it is known that more of Tippu's troops had died than Leopold's.

In 1887, after losing a great portion of his troops, Tippu Tib told the Sultan of Zanzibar to come to an agreement with the Belgian King and his agent, Henry Morton Stanley. This time, Leopold insisted on terms that would literally paralyze Tippu and the Sultan. Leopold made Tippu the governor of Stanley Falls again with the responsibility of keeping all the Arabs in the area in control but would not give him any weapons to do so. The local Arabs did not respect Tippu the same way after his alliance with Leopold and it became impossible for Tippu to maintain control.

By 1890, tired of the constant in fighting, Tippu returned to Zanzibar. Once there, he began preparations to leave for his homeland. At this time, the Force Publique attacked Zanzibar with decisive results. The Arab people were destroyed completely and the Sultan of Zanzibar agreed to the movement of the Belgians and the Force Publique across his country.

With Tippu Tib and Sultan of Zanzibar out of his way, Leopold established control over most of Central and Eastern Africa without ever stepping foot on the continent. Henry Morton Stanley, acting as his agent, had become the face of the war. But he was on the winning side. For the next 18 years, Leopold and Stanley had complete control over the Congo, a country where, till today, there are more valuable natural resources per square kilometre than anywhere else in the world. Leopold invested his gains to widen his personal coffers. Stanley retired with a mass of wealth greater than most monarchs. Belgium was at the forefront of the industrial revolution because of the massive investment of the obscene gains made by the plundering of the Congo Free State.

BELGIUM BEFORE LEOPOLD THE 2ND

The United Kingdom of the Netherlands had been established after the overthrow of Napoleonic rule in the region in 1813. The area known as the southern provinces (modern Belgium) had been offered to the Netherlands by the British in return for the handing over of Dutch Ceylon (Sri Lanka) and the Cape Colony (Cape of Good Hope in South Africa).

The Kingdom of Belgium acquired independence from the Dutch, following the French Revolutionary wars that culminated in to the Belgian Revolution of 1830. The causes of the revolution were economic, political and social. Over a period of 17 years, since amalgamation with the Netherlands, the people of the south-lying provinces rose up against their

Map of the Kingdom of Belgium

northern masters repeatedly but without much impact. Finally, in August 1830, the news of a successful uprising in France galvanised the people of Brussels. People took to the streets, occupied government buildings and rioting followed with nationalistic fervour. By the end of September 1830, a National Congress was summoned to draw up a Constitution and the provisional government was established. A Declaration of Independence followed on 4 October 1830.

King Leopold the 1st

In November 1830, the National Congress of Belgium was established to create a constitution for the new state.

The Congress decided that Belgium would be a popular, constitutional monarchy. On 7th February 1831, the Belgian Constitution was proclaimed. On 21st July, 1831, a German Prince named Leopold the 1st, who had taken commission to the Russian Imperial army and had fought against Napoleon, was selected as the King of Belgium. He was on good terms with the British Kingdom as he was married to Princess Charlotte of Wales, who was second in line to the British throne and the only legitimate child of the Prince Regent (the future King George IV).

For the first 8 years of his reign, he kept fighting off incursions by the Dutch from the north. He sought out assistance from the French who provided ample military support. In 1839, after many skirmishes, the Treaty of London was signed, under which the United Kingdom of Netherlands accepted the secession of Belgium and recognized as a separate nation, thus, officially heralding the existence of the Kingdom of Belgium.

Industrial Revolution

The fallout from the separation from the Netherlands did have a severe economic impact. The Port of Antwerp had become useless. Much of the trade in Belgium was dependent on the Dutch markets in the North. With the Treaty of London, Netherlands had basically cut off all economic ties with Belgium. There was mass migration of people from the smaller towns to the main cities and industrial centres. The Belgium economy faced a serious downturn that lasted till the early 1850s. But Leopold had the nous and foresight to understand that this would only be a temporary situation, if he planned for the future.

The Constitution of Belgium when first drafted, was rather loose in its terminology. Leopold amended it to afford more powers to the Monarch who ruled Belgium. With the expanded power, he decided to invest in the infrastructure of Belgium. By 1835, the first railway connecting Belgium to the rest of Europe was completed. With the industrial revolution spreading across Europe, he also commissioned the building of factories in the industrial areas of Belgium to create an unprecedented manufacturing ability for the country. Even though the economy was in depression and the agricultural production was failing, the future looked very bright.

Belgian Coat of Arms

The political situation was divided. The two main parties were the liberals and Catholics. Each party had their own agenda. The liberals were opposed to the Church's influence in politics and society, while supporting free trade, personal liberties and secularization. The Catholics wanted religious teachings to be a fundamental basis for the state and society and opposed all attempts by the liberals to attack the Church's official privileges. But neither party was an official organisation, hence, neither had any official bearing on the King's final decision. King Leopold was a protestant and he favoured the liberals but he could not oust the Catholics without inciting rebellion. This remained so till 1848, when during the elections the liberal party won by a significant majority and the Catholics were side-lined.

In 1848, the revolutionary environment had reached its precipice. There was a sentiment across nations to overthrown monarchy. Many Belgians living abroad returned home to overthrow the monarchy and establish a republic. But their efforts were swiftly thwarted by the Belgian armed forces. The monarchic rule of King Leopold the 1st continued.

Apart from the domestic popularity, King Leopold and his Belgium were widely respected by other nations as well. He was considered a great negotiator and one who promoted peace over violence. He had the reputation of being the mediator of international crisis during congregations of the influential powers of Europe. Because of his neutral stand, Belgium attained a reputation of a peace loving nation and was never deemed a threat to the other European powerhouses. King Leopold was popularly called the "Nestor of Europe", referring to the wise mediator Nestor from Homer's epic, The Iliad. He maintained good family ties with his many family members across Britain, France and Germany and avoided conflicts as much as he could, during his reign.

Till 1865, King Leopold had maintained peace in Belgium, created a stable political environment and set the foundation for rapid industrialization. Agriculture was thriving once again and the economy had moved out of depression had become stable. On 10th December, 1865, King Leopold the 1st passed away. He was succeeded by his second son, Leopold the 2nd.

> **BELGIUM'S POLITICAL CLIMATE**
>
> **Political State:** Imperial state, ruled by the King, and supported by the Holy Christian Church
>
> **Geographical Extent:** The Kingdom of Belgium was a newly independent territory, previously held by the Netherlands. Apart from the mainland, Belgium had only one colony, the Congo Free State.
>
> **Negotiation was preferred to war:** Belgium did not start nor did they participate in any war while they were under monarchic rule. Every time a conflict would occur, a negotiation was preferred to engaging the opponent. This was primarily because of the small military and naval forces of Belgium.
>
> **Colonization was promoted:** It was the era of the "Great Scramble for Africa". After an unsuccessful negotiation for Philippines for the queen of Spain, Leopold made repeated attempts to get an incursion into Congo sanctioned by the Belgian government to acquire Belgium's first colony.

BELGIUM UNDER LEOPOLD THE 2ND

Mission: To use his imperial position to build a large personal fortune, secure the longest reign of any Belgian King and the reputation of Belgium's great "Builder King"

King Leopold had wanted his son, Leopold the 2nd, to be prepared when he would ascend to the throne. He had sent his son to the army at a relatively young age. Leopold rose to the rank of lieutenant-general without ever having to fire a weapon. His royal lineage prevented him from ever entering a field of battle or picking up arms. He learnt the ways of the Belgian military till he was ready to be a part of the Belgian Senate. In 1855, when he reached majority age, he became a member of the Belgian Senate. He took an active interest in the workings of the Senate especially in matters concerning Belgium and its trade. He learnt about how to advance Belgian trade relationships with other nations and began to urge the acquisition of colonies for the country. For the next decade, he travelled extensively in the East, across Asia, and to the South, across the Mediterranean coasts of Africa.

LOBBYING FOR A COLONY, APPOINTING HENRY MORTON STANLEY AND LAYING THE FOUNDATION

7 days after the death of his father, Leopold the 2nd took the throne. As a monarch, he did not interfere with the local politics of Belgium. The Liberal party stayed in power for 15 years after Leopold took over and introduced many developments like free, secular and compulsory primary education schools and worker rights. In 1880, the Catholic party re-established majority but this was not very popular with the people. By 1885, the labour party came to power and they lobbied for worker rights once more for men, women and children. They also introduced voting rights for all men in Belgium.

Across Europe, at the time of his rule, the power of governance in many countries was being concentrated in the hands of the Senate. The same was happening in Belgium. The King could not be touched and neither could he be forced to leave his throne. As a result, King Leopold turned his attention towards his own personal project:

Acquiring a colony. Portugal, Spain, France and Britain had done so successfully across Asia, Africa and South America. Acquiring colonies had brought their respective monarchs great gains. King Leopold wanted to do the same. Even before he had ascended to the throne, he had wanted to acquire a colony using his power as a monarch to take a share of the great pool of resources in Asia and Africa.

King Leopold's repeated attempts to acquire the nation of Philippines in the past had been thwarted. He had negotiated with the Queen of Spain, Isabella the 2nd, to cede Philippines to his control. The negotiations had gone well, till they were completely stopped when Queen Isabella was deposed in 1868. He then tried to press his original plan to acquire the Philippines. But he was unsuccessful because of a lack of funds. Leopold then devised another unsuccessful plan to establish the Philippines as an independent state, which could then be ruled by a Belgian.

BELGIUM'S ECONOMIC PROFILE

Primary Work: Manufacturing and Export

Currency: Belgian Franc

Major Industries: Energy, rubber (export), textile, timber (export) and ivory (export)

Inexpensive import of raw materials: Because of the control over Congo, for almost 30 years, Belgium imported raw material for manufacturing at extremely low cost.

Large Scale Export: The Belgium economy had quickly adapted to supply ready made goods for export across the world. Belgium became one of the first nations to establish strong trade relations with the United States of America and Canada.

Low Unemployment: Under Leopold's reign, Belgium had recorded very low unemployment. In order to maintain a certain standard of the quality of the workplace, there were policies that were created for men, women and child workers.

Sizeable investment in infrastructure: Under Leopold, the Belgian government sought to invest heavily in the fortification of the country in case of future wars.

Henry Morton Stanley

In 1876, he heard of a journalist-explorer named Henry Morton Stanley who had explored the Congo River Basin and reported on its vast wealth of resources. He approached Stanley and proposed to

The Berlin Conference of 1885

him an opportunity to build the foundation to make Congo a colony of Belgium. Even though he was initially reluctant, Stanley finally agreed to his terms and began leading Belgian troops and builders to the Congo. The same year, King Leopold organised the International Geographic Conference in Brussels. The outcome of this conference was the founding of the International African Association (IAA), with Leopold II as its chairman, to undertake "altruistic and humanitarian projects in the area of Central Africa". Leopold II had also established the Commité d'Etudes du Haut-Congo (CEHC) under which Stanley was building outposts and a railway line from the heart of Congo (Kinshasa) to the Matadi, where the ships would make port. Stanley also made treaties with the local leaders in Congo, in order to use Congolese people as labour in exchange for a share of the gains.

Governor General Théophile Wahis

By 1885, the railway line was complete and the extraction of resources had begun but without the approval or recognition from the other European nation. At the Berlin conference of 1885, King Leopold made a strong argument for the work that he had commissioned in Congo and how he planned to further develop Congo. 14 European nations and the United States of America saw it in their favour to allow King Leopold to be sovereign of Congo. At the conference, International African Association was renamed the International Association of the Congo, the country was renamed to Congo Free State and King Leopold was given clearance to achieve his vision with Congo. As a result, Congo Free State, a land mass 76 times larger than Belgium, was established under King Leopold's personal rule.

FORCE PUBLIQUE, "RED RUBBER" AND "THE BUILDER KING"

King Leopold had created his own personal army to govern the Congo Free State. It was called the Force Publique. The army comprised of Belgian and other European mercenaries as officers, while the soldiers were a mix of African men of different tribes and nationalities. Till 1886, the officers reported to the Secretary of Interior, a post occupied by Henry Morton Stanley. In August 1886, a Belgian Army Captain named Leon Roger was named Commandant of the Force Publique by King Leopold. He had come to Congo a year ago and had decisively bolstered the ranks of the army. From then on till 1900, the officers reported to the Commandant. From 1900 till 1912, they reported to the Governor General of Congo Théophile Wahis. He reported directly to King Leopold and is known to have orchestrated the mass atrocities that were committed in Congo during his time.

Apart from keeping a strict eye on the daily work, the Force Publique also undertook exploration in the lands east of Congo in Central Africa. Because of these exploratory conquests, they were able to establish control over a land that was ceded by the British to Belgium called the Lado Enclave. The area was overrun by Arab slave traders and the rebels from the Middle East. The Force Publique fought them at different times between 1892 and 1897 and vanquished them from the area for good. The officers fortified themselves there and declared it a Belgian territory.

The officers were given jurisdictional powers as well. That is, they acted on their accord, without any legal authority to report to. They acted freely and without any supervision. Because of their brutality, the indigenous unarmed Congolese people were forced to work without remuneration. Their complaints or rebellions were met either with harsh punishment or death. Harsh punishments included starvation, induced disease, amputation, flogging and rape. As bonded labour, the natives had little choice but to cooperate with the Force Publique.

BELGIUM'S SOCIAL NORMS

Major Religion: Christianity was the most prominent religion as the Kingdom of Belgium had been founded with the blessing of the Christian clergy in Europe.

Language(s): Flemish, French and Dutch

Literature was promoted: The most prominent art form to flourish during Leopold's rule was literature. The art was promoted and writers and poets were revered in society.

Universal Male Suffrage: For the first time, all males within the political system were given the right to vote regardless of income, class, religion or race. But sometimes this resulted in one person voting more than once in an election.

Worker's rights: Children younger than 12 were not allowed to work in factories, children younger than 16 were not allowed to work at night. Women younger than 21 years old were not allowed to work in mines. Workers gained the right to be compensated for workplace accidents, and were given Sundays off.

Compulsory primary school education: Under the Frere-Orban Law of 1879, there was free, secular and compulsory primary schools supported by the state.

In Europe, Ivory was a very valuable commodity, as plastic did not exist at that time. Ivory was the most widely used material across all European nations and their colonies. By sourcing it from the Congo in unregulated, unmitigated quantities, under the tyranny of the Force Publique, Belgium became one of the few global suppliers of ivory. But the demand was not high at that point in time. Till 1890, the actual return was much lower than the expected return.

Cartoonist Edward Linley Sambourne depicts King Leopold II of Belgium as a snake entangling a Congolese rubber collector

By the early 1890s, a worldwide rubber boom was under way, kicked off by the invention of the inflatable bicycle tire and spurred on by the rise of the automobile, the use of rubber in industrial belts and gaskets, as well as in coating for telephone and telegraph wires. Throughout the tropics, people rushed to sow rubber trees, but those plants could take many years to reach maturity, and in the meantime there was money to be made wherever rubber grew wild. One lucrative source of wild rubber was the Landolphia vines in the great Central African rainforest, and no one owned more of that area than King Leopold.

King Leopold realized that in order to extract the large amounts of rubber that he needed to capture the global market, the natives had to work at a factory's pace. Extraction had to be streamlined. The officers had to be motivated to make the natives work even more. He announced target-based benefits to the officers. They in-turn became even more inhuman with the native workers. Driven by potential personal gains, the Force Publique raided villages and forced people to work, in exchange for their safety. The natives were helpless and they had to comply. This rubber was dubbed as

Edmund D. Morel

"Red Rubber" in the world media as the collection of rubber was covered with the blood of the natives.

Rubber became the main extract from Congo Free State. Secondary goods were timber and ivory. The roads and railway systems of Congo Free State were originally built in order to hasten the process of transporting goods from the interiors of the country to the ports. It was dubbed as the development of Congo's infrastructure, among other developmental activities for the country. All the gains from the extraction of these materials would be directly deposited in King Leopold's personal coffers. It is estimated that through the trade of these goods till 1908, King Leopold increased his personal wealth by as much as US$1.1 billion.

BELGIUM'S TECHNOLOGICAL ADVANCES

The Industrial Revolution: This revolution was one of the most dramatic milestones in the evolution of mankind. Belgium was at the forefront of adapting to this revolution and to benefit from it with swift creation of factories and capturing the lion's share of the global demand for many products and raw materials.

Establishing factories and railways: Before many other countries that had been the early adopters of industrialization, Belgium had built large factories that were capable of producing export quality goods. Along with that, Belgium became one of the first countries in the world to have a comprehensive railway network.

Sea voyages to import raw materials: While the naval forces of Belgium were almost negligible, once the natural resources from the Congo Free State were sourced, ships were rapidly built to facilitate movement of goods through sea voyages.

The atrocities committed to achieve this gain were noticed much after they had been committed. A British Journalist named Edmund D. Morel worked for almost 17 years to promote the reality of the "altruistic and humanitarian efforts in Congo" in the front page of the world news. This included reporting actual accounts from the region, publishing photographs of Congolese men, women and children whose limbs had been amputated by the Force Publique and evidence of scores of weapons and ammunitions being shipped to the Congo regularly for 17 years. In 1908, he was finally heard. The Belgian government began proceedings to remove King

Leopold as the sovereign of the Congo Free State.

The resolution of the matter would not be simple, though. A significant part of the monumental gains that King Leopold had made from Congo had been invested in many important public buildings urban projects and public works of Belgium. The public buildings were mainly in Brussels, Ostend and Antwerp. He expanded the grounds of the Royal Castle of Laeken, and built the Royal Greenhouses, the Japanese Tower and the Chinese Pavilion near the palace. In 1900, he created the Royal Trust, by means of which he donated most of his property to the Belgian nation, after his death. This preserved them to beautify Belgium in perpetuity, while still allowing future generations of the Belgian Royal family the privilege of their use.

In other countries, King Leopold was also highly revered. He had close ties with many other European nations which allowed them to remain neutral on many issues. Like his father, he kept Belgium out of all serious conflicts between their allies and always maintaining the position of a peaceful mediator. Because of this reputation, his reign was never challenged by other imperial powers and he was a highly decorated King. He had established good trade relations with almost all of Europe and their colonies. He had been honoured with 63 honorary imperial titles by 42 countries.

For all practical purposes, he was the King that Belgium needed to further the nation's ambition to become a modern and developed nation. King Leopold was the one responsible for them being at the forefront of the industrial revolution. He had stabilized the economy and brought great gains to the nation. He had invested his wealth for the betterment of the Belgian people. Apart from his deplorable habit of spending lavishly on under age prostitutes, his image was one of a visionary king who cared for Belgium. Among the common people, he was called the "Builder King".

Even though the Catholic and Liberal party were outraged by the atrocities he had committed, they were a part of a developed economy because of the investment of his wealth. They offered to pay him US$1.5 million to concede the territory of Congo to the Belgian government. Even though this was a paltry sum of money compared to his actual gains, an aging King Leopold accepted the offer and conceded Congo Free State to them on 15th November, 1908.

After conceding the Congo Free State to the Belgian Government and his death in the year of 1909, there occurred a "Great Forgetting". Systematically, many evidences of the King's atrocities were erased and in their place were installed new monuments and commemorations that celebrated him as a great King who brought the gift of civilization to the Congo Free State. Both in Congo and Belgium, many have gone to great lengths to preserve a different legacy of the King. Till today, there are grand structures and buildings that show King Leopold as a benevolent and caring leader. Thus, many of the 20th and 21st century do not even know about the holocaust caused by King Leopold.

STRENGTH-WEAKNESS-OPPORTUNITY-THREAT (SWOT) ANALYSIS OF KING LEOPOLD THE 2ND

STRENGTHS	WEAKNESSES
"The Builder King": During the later years of his life, Leopold came to be known as "The Builder King" of Belgium because of the large number of buildings, urban projects and public works he built with his astronomical earnings from the exploitation of Congo. Till today, the cognomen is associated with him, despite his gross violations of human rights in the African country. **Intelligent Diplomat:** Leopold was born to royal blood and he acted the same way. He maintained good relationships with the monarchs and Kaisers of neighbouring nations, even during times of conflict and war, which resulted 63 honorary titles bestowed upon him by 42 nations, dynasties, Empires and Kingdoms **Opportunist:** Leopold capitalized on profitable opportunities throughout his reign. This included negotiating profitable terms with other monarchs and investing in profitable ventures.	**Greedy:** Leopold had a strong penchant for desiring more than he needed. The plan of destroying Congo was borne out of his desire to match the colonies of other European nations, even though Belgium did not have the resources to undertake colonization. His greed also led to the annihilation of half of a country's population in the pursuit of extracting ivory and rubber. **Abhorrent:** Because of his imperial status, he was the subject of many rumours. Further, his actions gave substantial credence to many such rumours about his inhuman treatment of people of colour and his paedophilic tendencies. **Insecurity:** The Kingdom of Belgium had come into existence with his father, Leopold the 1st and was a relatively small country with no major influence in Europe. Leopold had always lived under the shadow of this fact and he wanted to have the might of the other nations. His ambitions stemmed from his need to boast of his achievements to other monarchs, not from the need to make Belgium stronger as a nation
OPPORTUNITIES	**THREATS**
Modernization of the Kingdom of Belgium: When he took over as King, Leopold had the opportunity to invest for the development of Belgium. The country became one of the first countries in the world to feel the effects of the industrial revolution with large manufacturing facilities being setup under Leopold's orders. **To capture a colony, like other Imperial powers:** It was the going trend for European powers to acquire colonies of Africa at that point in time. It was called the "Great Scramble for Africa". **To establish a monopoly in natural resources from Congo:** Congo was known to be rich in natural resources and with no other nation vying for Congo, Leopold established a monopoly in the extraction and sale of resources like rubber and ivory. **To cement his reputation as a Great King:** With the almost-infinite gains from the sourcing of rubber and ivory, Leopold invest a part of those profits in building grand structures and fortifications for the country, thus, establishing his reputation as the great "Builder King".	**International dissention for his deplorable acts in Congo:** By the early 1900s, the details of the gruesome and inhuman treatment of the Congolese people had become known to the world. Since then, there were repeated prosecution of Leopold and his methods till the Belgian government took over Congo in 1908. **Internal rebellion against his extreme methods in Congo:** Throughout his time, it was highly probable that the Congolese people would rebel against Leopold's troops in Congo. This happened occasionally. But each time, the rebellion had been quelled without much damage. **Attacks from the Arabs in Congo:** Leopold's forced acquisition of the Congo had disturbed the Arab slave market that had existed there much before his arrival. After repeated negotiations and confrontations, the Arabs were comprehensively defeated by the Force Publique in the Battle of Rejaf.

WHY IS LEOPOLD THE 2ND AN AUTOCRATIC LEADER?

An autocratic leader is one who holds undisputed autonomous power. An autocratic leader is one whose decisions are considered final and are to be followed in absolution. Autocratic leaders reach decisions, communicate them to subordinates and expect prompt implementation. Leopold the 2nd fit the bill of such a leader completely. In Belgium, where he was King, and in Congo, where he was the sovereign leader, there was no one to dispute his authority. Leopold used this power to complete effect, but in contrasting ways.

In Belgium, he gathered the support of his people by being hailed as the "Builder King" who invested in the construction of many long lasting buildings and structures for the people. Even though he wasn't a benevolent leader, his decisions to beautify Belgium and embrace the industrial revolution won him great favour among the Belgians. His decision to modernize Belgium allowed him to be the longest serving Monarch in the history of Belgium. It also led to Belgians turning a blind eye to the atrocities committed many miles away in Congo.

In Congo, on the other hand, he was the autocratic ruler who did not want to win over any of the Congolese people. He wanted to extract as much wealth as he possibly could in the 23 years he was given a free hand in the country. He exploited the people and destroyed the country, both economically and socially. Under his rule, Belgium became the world's largest supplier of ivory, rubber and timber in the world,

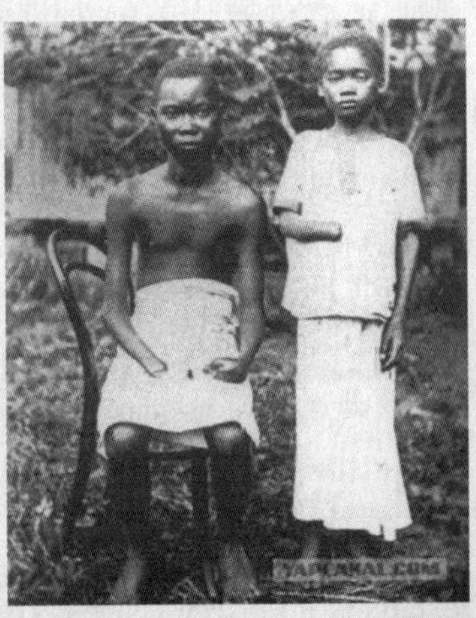

Two Congolese youth with amputated hands

all of which was sourced from Congo. The Congolese people were massacred by an ultra-violent mercenary unit called the Force Publique, which was installed by Leopold to quell any disturbance and kill anyone who would stop or protest against the exploitation. In Congo, Leopold committed some of the worst atrocities known to mankind.

His autocratic nature stemmed from the validation he received for his decisions as a monarch. In essence, he was in a position to get away with anything he did and he took advantage of this opportunity as best as he could. Leopold was honoured by 42 nations with 63 titles at the same time as he was committing the crimes against humanity in Congo. He gained great wealth and large estates because of his position. As an autocratic ruler, he heavily advanced the economic condition of Belgium by capitalizing on the lack of development and industrialization in Congo.

LEOPOLD'S DEATH

When he was forced to hand over Congo to the Belgian government, he was overcome with the worry that the atrocities and inhuman activities conducted in the African nation under his command would become public information. He had all the archives and paperwork of his deeds destroyed before officials of the Belgian government reached Congo. But his deeds had already become public news (through photographs and books) and he was harshly criticized by many across the European continent.

During his last year, it is said that King Leopold became cynical. He also became eccentric and lavished astonishing gifts on his favourite mistress, Caroline Lacroix, a 25 year old French prostitute. He married her in a Christian ceremony 5 days before he died and in his will, left a sum of US$7,000,000 in her name, which became a topic of serious controversy among Leopold's children. On 17th December, 1909, he died of a cerebral haemorrhage, under the care of his new wife.

There were rumours that it had been Caroline Lacroix's plan all along to secure her inheritance in his will and then dispose of him.

When his funeral carriage transported his body through the streets of Brussels, there was loud symphony of boos from the public who were glad to be rid of their much-maligned King. The public's hatred for their King did not stem from the atrocities he committed in the Congo Free State. They stemmed from their disapproval of his acts of debauchery and paedophilic tendencies.

LEOPOLD'S LAST KNOWN LOCATION

Leopold's remains were interred in the royal vault of the Church of Our Lady of Laeken in Brussels, Belgium.

LEOPOLD'S FINAL KILL COUNT

There is a problem in counting the actual number of people killed in the atrocities committed in the Congo Free State under the rule of Leopold. Writers, missionaries and anthropologists have been unable to make a clear and undisputed estimation of the number of people who had been slaughtered under Leopold's rule. This is so because genocide is not the only known sources of death during Leopold's reign. Many thousands (hundreds of thousands) also died because of the inhuman conditions they had to live in. Communicable diseases like small pox, malaria and sleeping sickness also gathered an enormous death toll, apart from the deaths by execution.

During his control of Congo, from 1885 to 1908, Leopold ordered the mass eradication of Congolese people who would impede the extraction of ivory, rubber and timber. The liberty he gave the Force Publique allowed them to kill or mutilate people as per their will, whim or judgment. This included cutting off hands and feet of men, women and children. The estimated range of people that were killed during Leopold's reign of terror in Congo is 10-15 million people, in a country where there were approximately 20-22 million people at the turn of the end of the 19th century.

ABOUT THE AUTHOR

Anurag Sikder is a writer based in New Delhi, India. He is a trained and experienced professional who has worked with numerous media and research organisations. Apart from research-based texts, Anurag is a script writer for stage, film and television.